BOOK 1 - Drums & Mallet Percussion

STANDARD OF EXCELLENCE

COMPREHENSIVE BAND METHOD

By Bruce Pearson

Dear Student:

Welcome to the wonderful world of instrumental music. The moment you pick up your drum sticks and mallets, you will begin an exciting adventure that is filled with challenges and rewards. If you study carefully and practice regularly, you will quickly discover the joy and satisfaction of playing beautiful music for yourself, your family, your friends, or a concert audience.

I hope you have many rewarding years of music-making.

Best wishes,

Bruce Pearson

Practicing - the key to EXCELLENCE!

▶ Make practicing part of your daily schedule. If you plan it as you do any other activity, you will find plenty of time for it.
▶ Try to practice in the same place every day. Choose a place where you can concentrate on making music. Start with a regular and familiar warm-up routine, including rudiments and simple technical exercises. Like an athlete, you need to warm-up your mind and muscles before you begin performing.
▶ Set goals for every practice session. Keep track of your practice time and progress on the front cover Practice Journal.
▶ Practice the hard spots in your lesson assignment and band music over and over, until you can play them perfectly.
▶ Spend time practicing both alone and with the STANDARD OF EXCELLENCE recorded accompaniments. Make time for practice on both snare drum and your mallet percussion instrument.
▶ At the end of each practice session, play something fun.

Also Available: STANDARD OF EXCELLENCE Timpani & Auxiliary Percussion, Book 1 (W21TM)

ISBN 0-8497-5945-5

KJOS NEIL A. KJOS MUSIC COMPANY, PUBLISHER

W21PR

PUTTING YOUR SNARE DRUM TOGETHER

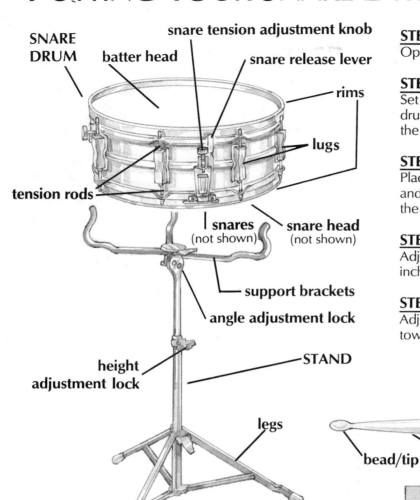

SNARE DRUM

batter head

snare tension adjustment knob

snare release lever

rims

lugs

tension rods

snares (not shown)

snare head (not shown)

support brackets

angle adjustment lock

height adjustment lock

STAND

legs

STEP 1
Open your case right side up.

STEP 2
Set up the stand so that it rests solidly on the floor. The three drum support brackets should be spread out and level with the floor.

STEP 3
Place the drum on the stand so that the snares face the floor and the snare release lever is directly in front of you. Adjust the drum support arms to hold the drum snugly in place.

STEP 4
Adjust the stand height so that the top rim of the drum is four inches below your waist.

STEP 5
Adjust the angle of the stand so that the drum leans slightly toward you.

DRUM STICK

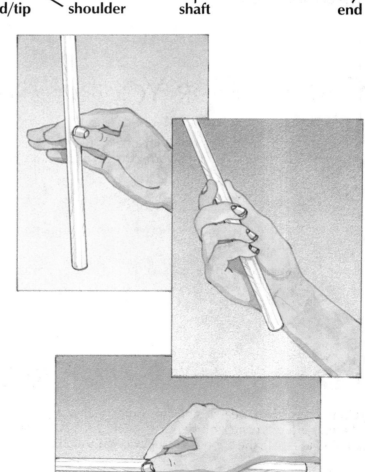

bead/tip   **shoulder**   **shaft**   **end**

PREPARING TO PLAY

STEP 1
Stand up straight with your feet slightly spread and your weight distributed evenly on both feet.

STEP 2
Bend your arm at the elbow and lift your hand until your forearm is at a slight angle to the floor.

STEP 3
Find the spot on the drum stick approximately one-third of the length from the end. Place that part of the stick between the first joint of your index finger and the pad of your thumb.

STEP 4
Place your remaining fingers on the stick and pull it in toward your palm. Your fingers should hold the stick loosely, and your thumb should point toward the drum stick tip. Your palm should face down when the stick is parallel to the drum head.

STEP 5
Repeat steps two through four with your other hand.

PLAYING YOUR SNARE DRUM

STEP 1
Stand about eight inches from your drum with your feet comfortably apart and your weight equally placed on each foot. Hold the sticks using the correct grip.

STEP 2
Hold your sticks one to two inches above and almost parallel to the batter head. The sticks should form a 60 degree angle.

STEP 3
Using your wrist, raise the tip of the stick six to eight inches above the head. Then, drop the tip of the stick to the head and allow it to bounce off. The stick should strike the head slightly off-center directly above the snares.

STEP 4
To follow immediately with another stroke in the same hand, allow the stick to rebound six to eight inches above the drum head, then play the next stroke. To pause between strokes, allow the stick to rebound to its rest position one to two inches above the drum head (step 2).

STEP 5
When striking the drum, imagine that you are drawing the tone out of the drum.

CARING FOR YOUR SNARE DRUM

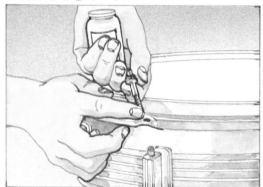

STEP 1
Clean the drum heads regularly with a damp cloth. Replace the heads when they become worn, dented, or punctured.

STEP 2
Periodically clean metal parts and hoops with a damp cloth or metal polish.

STEP 3
Periodically lubricate tension rods with petroleum jelly or light grease. Lubricate the snare strainer and other moving parts with household machine oil or lubricant.

PLAYING THE BASS DRUM

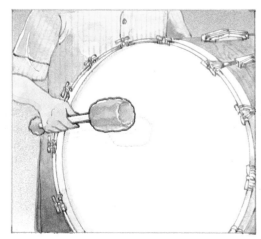

Using a bass drum beater, strike the drum halfway between the rim and the center of the head. Use a direct forearm motion to create the stroke (not a glancing motion).

PUTTING YOUR MALLET PERCUSSION INSTRUMENT TOGETHER

BELLS
(MALLET INSTRUMENT)

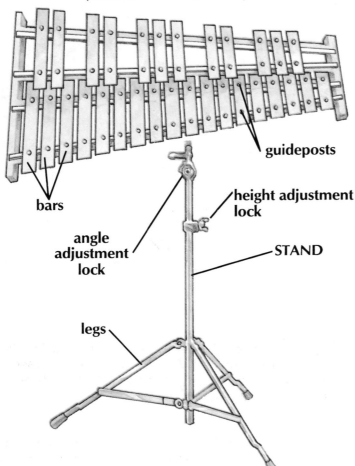

bars

guideposts

angle adjustment lock

height adjustment lock

STAND

legs

STEP 1
Open your case right side up.

STEP 2
Set up the stand so that it rests solidly on the floor.

STEP 3
Place the mallet instrument securely on the stand with the larger bars to your left.

STEP 4
Adjust the stand height so that the mallet instrument is four inches below your waist.

STEP 5
Position the music stand just above the bars so that you can see the music and the bars at the same time.

MALLET

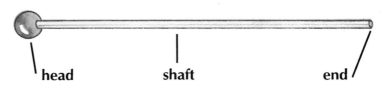

head　　　　　shaft　　　　　end

PREPARING TO PLAY

STEP 1
Stand up straight with your feet slightly spread and your weight distributed evenly on both feet.

STEP 2
Bend your arm at the elbow and lift your hand until your forearm is at a slight angle to the floor.

STEP 3
Find the spot on the mallet approximately one-third of the length from the end. Place that part of the mallet between the first joint of your index finger and the pad of your thumb.

STEP 4
Place your remaining fingers on the mallet and pull it in toward your palm. Your fingers should hold the mallet loosely, and your thumb should point toward the mallet head. Your palm should face down when the mallet is parallel to the mallet instrument.

STEP 5
Repeat steps two through four with your other hand.

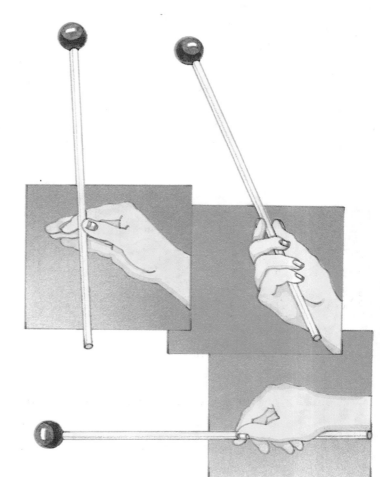

PLAYING YOUR MALLET PERCUSSION INSTRUMENT

STEP 1
Stand about eight inches from your mallet percussion instrument with your feet comfortably apart and your weight equally placed on each foot. Hold the mallets using the correct grip.

STEP 2
Position the music stand just above the bars so you can see the music and the bars at the same time. Hold your mallets two to three inches above and almost parallel with the bars; keep your hands low.

STEP 3
Using your wrist, raise the head of the mallet six to eight inches above the bar. Then, strike the bar with a quick down-up motion. Strike the bar in the center. Raised bars may be struck in the center or on the ends.

STEP 4
To follow immediately with another stroke in the same hand, return the mallet to its position six to eight inches above the bar, then play the next stroke. To pause between strokes, return the mallet to its rest position two to three inches above the bar (step 2).

STEP 5
When striking a bar, imagine that you are drawing the tone out of the bar. When playing two notes in a row on the same bar, position one mallet (usually the left) in front of the other.

CARING FOR YOUR MALLET PERCUSSION INSTRUMENT

STEP 1
Dust off the bars regularly with a soft cloth.

STEP 2
Check regularly to see that the bars are not binding against the guideposts.

STEP 3
Cover your mallet percussion instrument when not in use.

FOR SNARE DRUMS & PERCUSSION ONLY

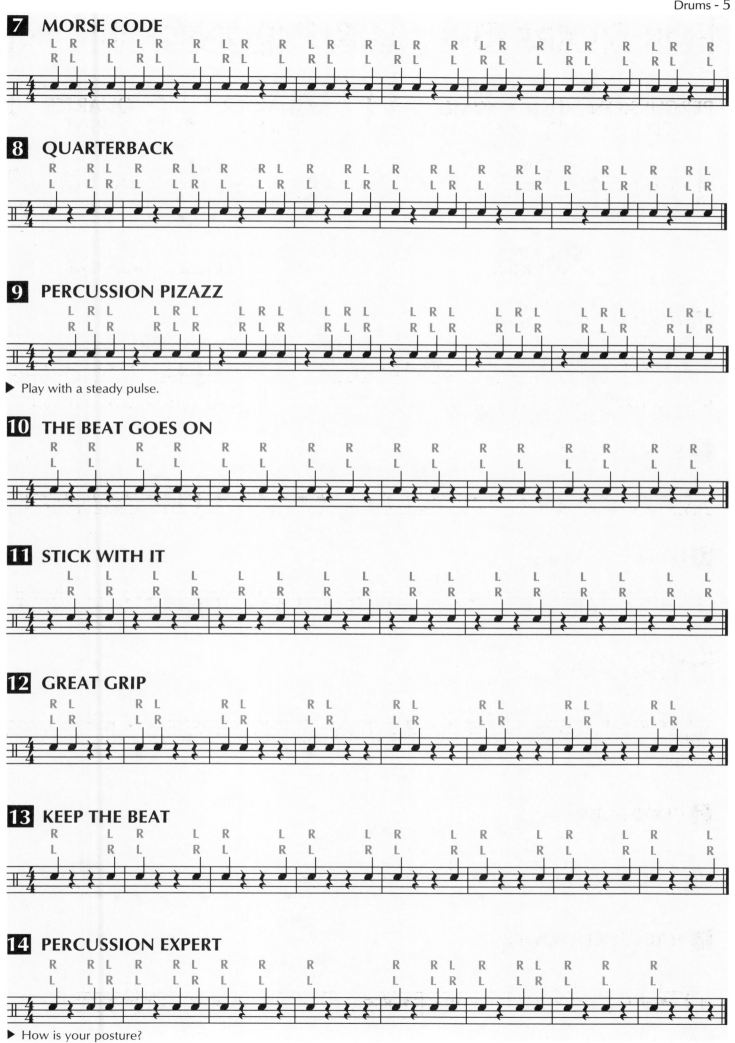

▶ Play with a steady pulse.

▶ How is your posture?

FOR MALLETS & PERCUSSION ONLY

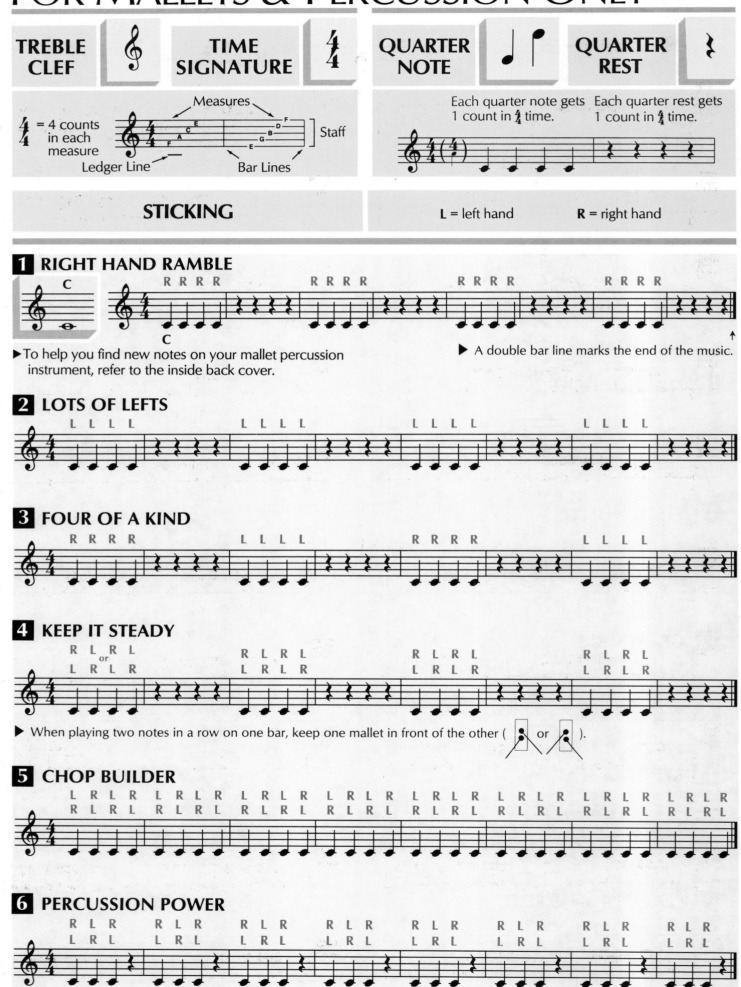

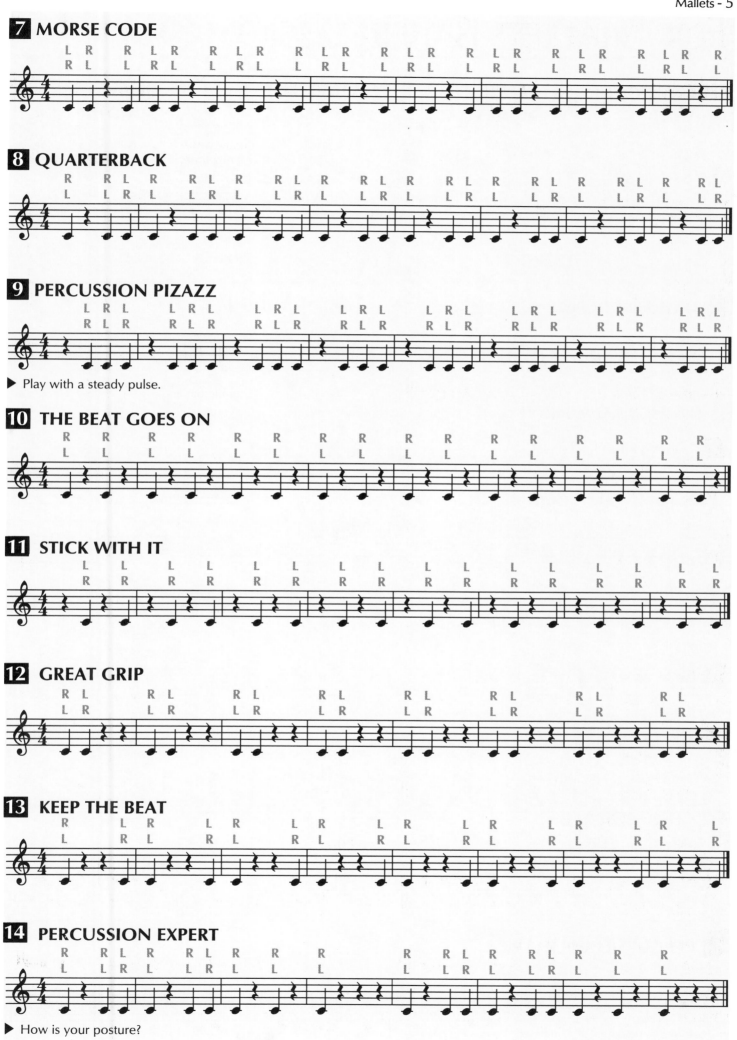

7 MORSE CODE

8 QUARTERBACK

9 PERCUSSION PIZAZZ

▶ Play with a steady pulse.

10 THE BEAT GOES ON

11 STICK WITH IT

12 GREAT GRIP

13 KEEP THE BEAT

14 PERCUSSION EXPERT

▶ How is your posture?

FOR THE FULL BAND

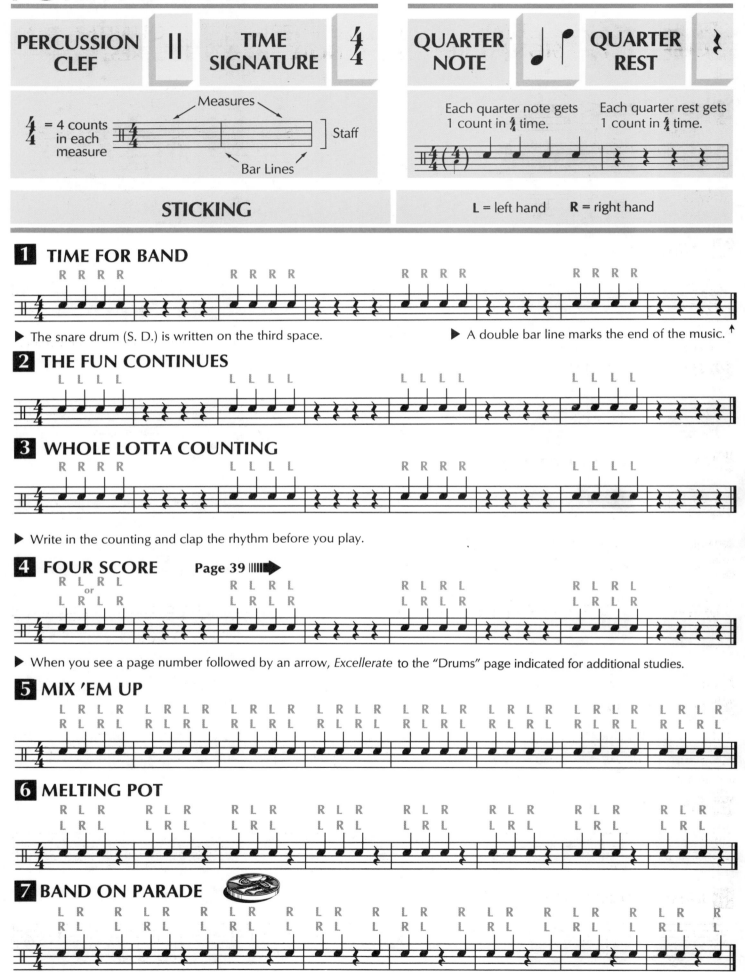

PERCUSSION CLEF ‖ **TIME SIGNATURE** 𝄴 **QUARTER NOTE** ♩ ♩ **QUARTER REST** 𝄽

4/4 = 4 counts in each measure — Measures — Staff — Bar Lines

Each quarter note gets 1 count in 4/4 time. Each quarter rest gets 1 count in 4/4 time.

STICKING — L = left hand   R = right hand

1 TIME FOR BAND
R R R R   R R R R   R R R R   R R R R

▶ The snare drum (S. D.) is written on the third space.   ▶ A double bar line marks the end of the music.

2 THE FUN CONTINUES
L L L L   L L L L   L L L L   L L L L

3 WHOLE LOTTA COUNTING
R R R R   L L L L   R R R R   L L L L

▶ Write in the counting and clap the rhythm before you play.

4 FOUR SCORE   Page 39 ‖‖‖▶
R L R L or L R L R   R L R L / L R L R   R L R L / L R L R   R L R L / L R L R

▶ When you see a page number followed by an arrow, *Excellerate* to the "Drums" page indicated for additional studies.

5 MIX 'EM UP
L R L R (×8) / R L R L (×8)

6 MELTING POT
R L R / L R L (repeated)

7 BAND ON PARADE
L R R L R / R L L R L (repeated)

▶ Lines with a medal are *Achievement Lines*. The chart on "Drums" page 47 can be used to record your progress.

FOR THE FULL BAND

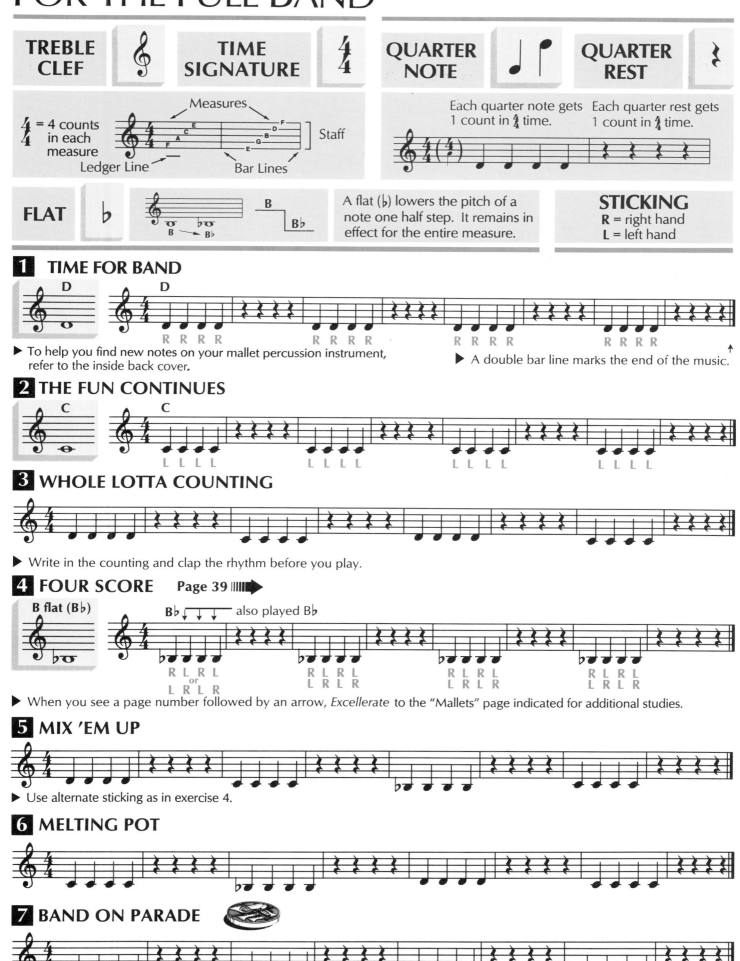

TREBLE CLEF

TIME SIGNATURE $\frac{4}{4}$

QUARTER NOTE

QUARTER REST

$\frac{4}{4}$ = 4 counts in each measure

Measures

Ledger Line

Bar Lines

Staff

Each quarter note gets 1 count in $\frac{4}{4}$ time.

Each quarter rest gets 1 count in $\frac{4}{4}$ time.

FLAT ♭

B → B♭

B♭

A flat (♭) lowers the pitch of a note one half step. It remains in effect for the entire measure.

STICKING
R = right hand
L = left hand

1 TIME FOR BAND

D

D

R R R R   R R R R   R R R R   R R R R

▶ To help you find new notes on your mallet percussion instrument, refer to the inside back cover.

▶ A double bar line marks the end of the music.

2 THE FUN CONTINUES

C

C

L L L L   L L L L   L L L L   L L L L

3 WHOLE LOTTA COUNTING

▶ Write in the counting and clap the rhythm before you play.

4 FOUR SCORE   Page 39 ▶

B flat (B♭)

B♭   also played B♭

R L R L   R L R L   R L R L   R L R L
or
L R L R   L R L R   L R L R   L R L R

▶ When you see a page number followed by an arrow, *Excellerate* to the "Mallets" page indicated for additional studies.

5 MIX 'EM UP

▶ Use alternate sticking as in exercise 4.

6 MELTING POT

7 BAND ON PARADE

▶ Lines with a medal are *Achievement Lines*. The chart on "Mallets" page 47 can be used to record your progress.

HALF NOTE | **HALF REST**

Each half note gets 2 counts in 4/4 time. Each half rest gets 2 counts in 4/4 time.

8 A BREATH OF FRESH AIR

9 SIDE BY SIDE

10 TWO BY TWO

11 HALF THE PRICE

▶ Write in the counting and clap the rhythm before you play.

12 CARDIFF BY THE SEA   Page 39 ▶   Welsh Folk Song

13 TWO FOR THE SHOW - Duet

14 GO FOR EXCELLENCE!

SINGLE PARADIDDLE

Rudiments are the basic techniques and sticking patterns used in snare drum playing. The single paradiddle is a Rudiment.

WHOLE NOTE o **WHOLE REST** ▬

A whole note gets 4 counts in $\frac{4}{4}$ time.

A whole rest gets 4 counts in $\frac{4}{4}$ time.

PHRASE A phrase is a musical thought or sentence. Phrases are usually four or eight measures long.

15 A QUARTER'S WORTH
Single Paradiddle

▶ Write in the counting and clap the rhythm before you play.

16 HOT CROSS BUNS
English Folk Song

17 AU CLAIRE DE LA LUNE
French Folk Song

▶ Draw in a breath mark (') at the end of each phrase.

18 DOWN BY THE STATION
Traditional

19 EASY STREET

20 COUNTRY WALK
English Folk Song

21 GETTIN' IT TOGETHER

22 FOR SNARE DRUMS ONLY

W21PR

| WHOLE NOTE | o | WHOLE REST | – | PHRASE |

A whole note gets 4 counts in 4/4 time.

A whole rest gets 4 counts in 4/4 time.

A phrase is a musical thought or sentence. Phrases are usually four or eight measures long.

15 A QUARTER'S WORTH

▶ Write in the counting and clap the rhythm before you play.

16 HOT CROSS BUNS

English Folk Song

clap

17 AU CLAIRE DE LA LUNE

French Folk Song

▶ Draw in a breath mark (') at the end of each phrase.

18 DOWN BY THE STATION

Traditional

19 EASY STREET

E flat (E♭)

E♭

20 COUNTRY WALK

English Folk Song

21 GETTIN' IT TOGETHER

F

F

22 FOR MALLETS ONLY

L R L R L R L R L R L R L R R L L L

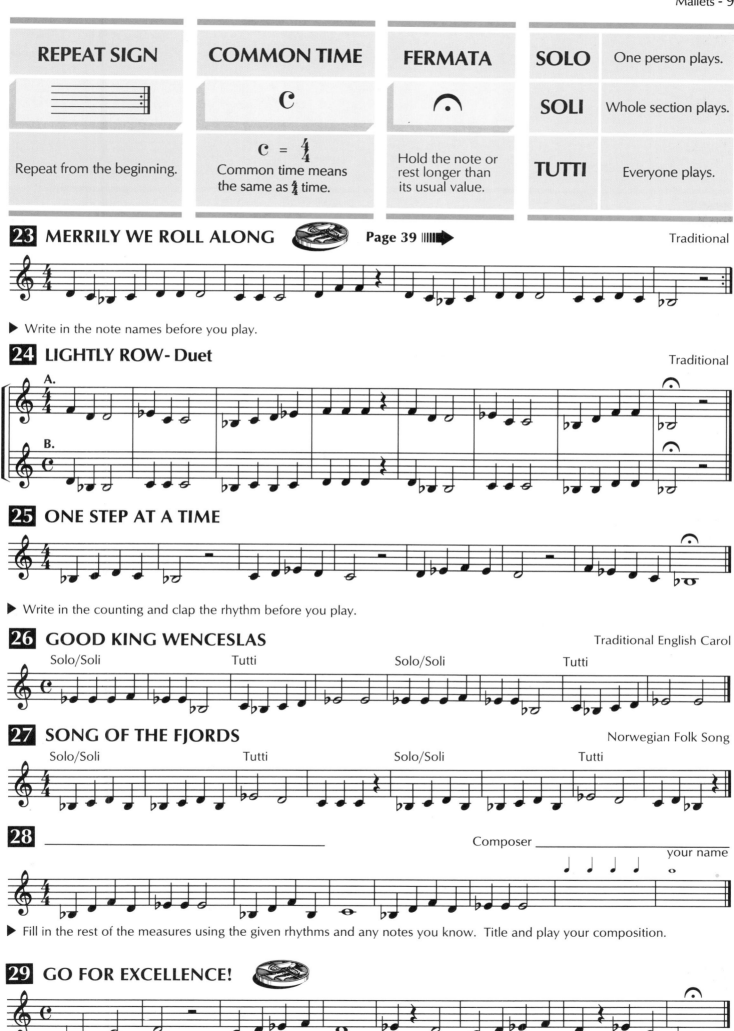

REPEAT SIGN

Repeat from the beginning.

COMMON TIME

C

C = 4/4

Common time means the same as 4/4 time.

FERMATA

Hold the note or rest longer than its usual value.

SOLO — One person plays.

SOLI — Whole section plays.

TUTTI — Everyone plays.

23 MERRILY WE ROLL ALONG Page 39 ▶

Traditional

▶ Write in the note names before you play.

24 LIGHTLY ROW - Duet

Traditional

A.

B.

25 ONE STEP AT A TIME

▶ Write in the counting and clap the rhythm before you play.

26 GOOD KING WENCESLAS

Traditional English Carol

Solo/Soli   Tutti   Solo/Soli   Tutti

27 SONG OF THE FJORDS

Norwegian Folk Song

Solo/Soli   Tutti   Solo/Soli   Tutti

28 _____   Composer _____

your name

▶ Fill in the rest of the measures using the given rhythms and any notes you know. Title and play your composition.

29 GO FOR EXCELLENCE!

TIE

A tie is a curved line that connects two notes on the <u>same</u> line or space. Tied notes are played as one unbroken note.

TIME SIGNATURE

$\frac{2}{4}$

$\frac{2}{4}$ = 2 counts in each measure
= quarter note gets one count

30 WARM-UP

31 TIED AND TRUE

Page 39 ▶

32 JOLLY OLD ST. NICHOLAS - Duet

American Carol

A. S.D.

B.D.

B. S.D.

S.D. (snares off)

33 AMIGOS

Mexican Folk Song

▶ Keep on playing!

▶ Write in the counting and clap the rhythm before you play.

34 FARM OUT

Traditional

35 FOR SNARE DRUMS ONLY

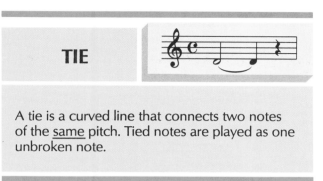

TIE

A tie is a curved line that connects two notes of the <u>same</u> pitch. Tied notes are played as one unbroken note.

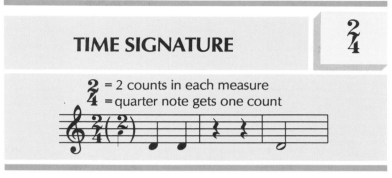

TIME SIGNATURE

$\frac{2}{4}$ = 2 counts in each measure
$\frac{2}{4}$ = quarter note gets one count

30 WARM-UP

31 TIED AND TRUE

32 JOLLY OLD ST. NICHOLAS - Duet

American Carol

A.

B.

33 AMIGOS   Page 40 ||||▶

Mexican Folk Song

▶ Keep on playing!

▶ Write in the counting and clap the rhythm before you play.

34 FARM OUT

Traditional

35 FOR MALLETS ONLY

L R L R   L R   L R L R L R   L   R   L R L R L R   R L R L   R   L

11 - Drums

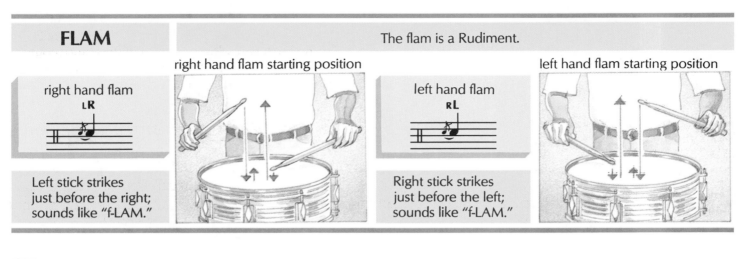

FLAM

The flam is a Rudiment.

36 MARK TIME

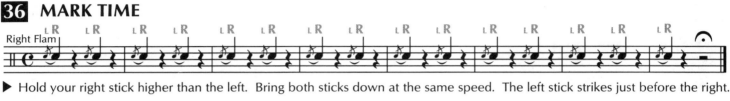

▶ Hold your right stick higher than the left. Bring both sticks down at the same speed. The left stick strikes just before the right.

37 SWEETLY SINGS THE DONKEY - Round

Traditional

▶ Hold your left stick higher than the right. Bring both sticks down at the same speed. The right stick strikes just before the left.

38 MARY ANN

West Indies Folk Song

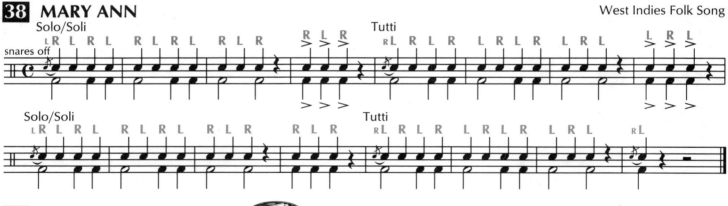

39 CRUSADER'S MARCH

Traditional

▶ Write in the counting and clap the rhythm before you play.

40 BALANCE THE SCALES ▶ See "Mallets" page 11.

41 GO FOR EXCELLENCE!

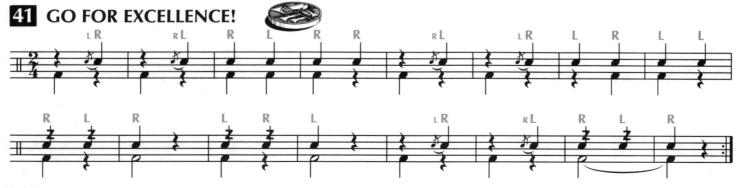

KEY SIGNATURE

Key signatures change certain notes throughout a piece of music. This key signature means play all B's as B flats and all E's as E flats.

36 MARK TIME

37 SWEETLY SINGS THE DONKEY - Round

Traditional

38 MARY ANN

West Indies Folk Song

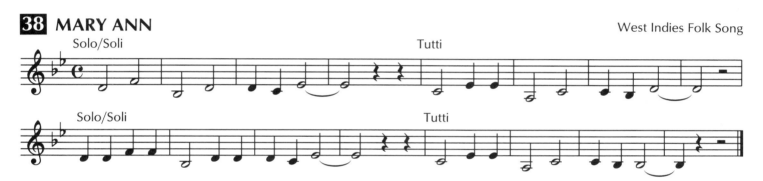

▶ Write in the note names before you play.

39 CRUSADER'S MARCH Page 40 ▐▐▐▶

Traditional

▶ Write in the counting and clap the rhythm before you play.

40 BALANCE THE SCALES

Draw *one* note or *one* rest to balance each scale.

41 GO FOR EXCELLENCE!

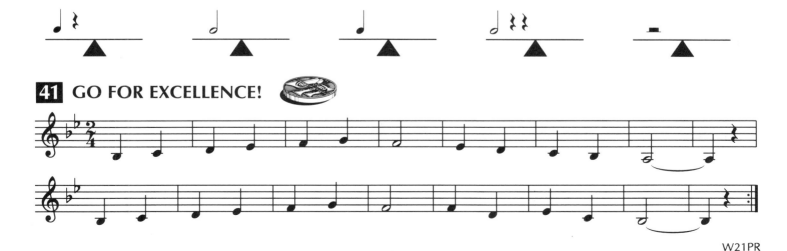

FLAM TAP

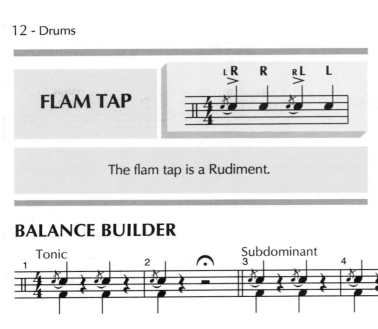

The flam tap is a Rudiment.

ONE-MEASURE REPEAT SIGN

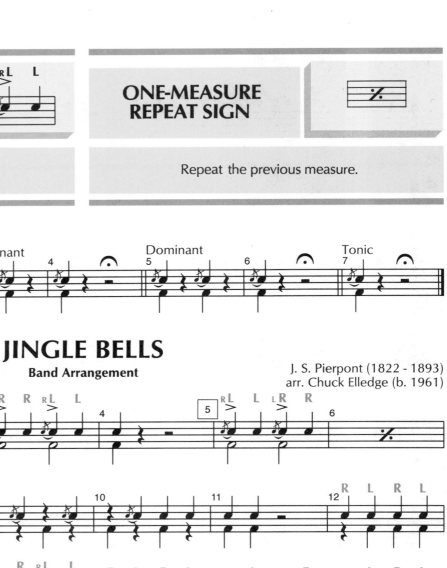

Repeat the previous measure.

BALANCE BUILDER

JINGLE BELLS
Band Arrangement

J. S. Pierpont (1822 - 1893)
arr. Chuck Elledge (b. 1961)

42 SCHOOL SONG   Page 39 Page 39

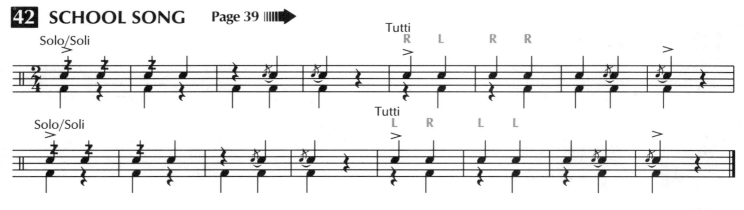

43 FOR SNARE DRUMS ONLY

BALANCE BUILDER

JINGLE BELLS
Band Arrangement

J. S. Pierpont (1822 - 1893)
arr. Chuck Elledge (b. 1961)

42 SCHOOL SONG

43 FOR MALLETS ONLY

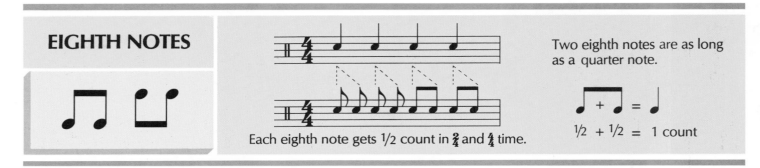

EIGHTH NOTES

Two eighth notes are as long as a quarter note.

Each eighth note gets ½ count in $\frac{2}{4}$ and $\frac{4}{4}$ time.

½ + ½ = 1 count

44 WARM-UP

45 EIGHTH NOTE ENCOUNTER

▶ Write in the counting before you play.

46 JIM ALONG JOSIE

American Folk Song

47 EIGHTH NOTE EXPLORER

▶ Write in the counting before you play.

48 GO TELL BILL

Gioacchino Rossini (1792–1868)

49 GO FOR EXCELLENCE!

EIGHTH NOTES

Two eighth notes are as long as a quarter note.

Each eighth note gets ½ count in 2/4 and 4/4 time.

½ + ½ = 1 count

44 WARM-UP

45 EIGHTH NOTE ENCOUNTER

clap

▶ Write in the counting for the top line before you play.

46 JIM ALONG JOSIE

American Folk Song

47 EIGHTH NOTE EXPLORER

clap

▶ Write in the counting for the top line before you play.

48 GO TELL BILL

Gioacchino Rossini (1792 - 1868)

49 GO FOR EXCELLENCE!

50 EIGHTH NOTE EXPRESS

▶ Write in the counting before you play.

51 SKIP IT, LOU

American Folk Song

Solo/Soli   Tutti

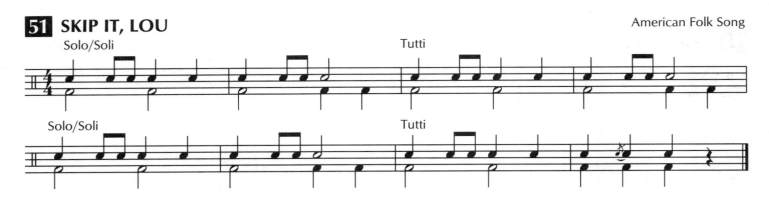

Solo/Soli   Tutti

52 EIGHTH NOTE EXPERT

▶ Write in the counting before you play.

53 MEXICAN MOUNTAIN SONG

Page 39 ▶

Mexican Folk Song

54 BAFFLING BAR LINES

▶ Write in the counting and draw in the bar lines before you play.

55 FOR SNARE DRUMS ONLY

50 EIGHTH NOTE EXPRESS

▶ Write in the counting for the top line before you play.

51 SKIP IT, LOU

American Folk Song

52 EIGHTH NOTE EXPERT

▶ Write in the counting for the top line before you play.

53 MEXICAN MOUNTAIN SONG   Page 40 ▶

Mexican Folk Song

54 BAFFLING BAR LINES

▶ Write in the counting and draw in the bar lines before you play.

55 FOR MALLETS ONLY

Do all of your strokes sound the same?

PICK-UP NOTE

A note that comes before the first full measure of a piece of music.

56 WARM-UP

57 THEME FROM "SYMPHONY NO. 1" — Johannes Brahms (1833 - 1897)

58 ERIE CANAL CAPERS — American Work Song

59 LAUGHING SONG - Round — Traditional

60 STAR SEARCH — Wolfgang Amadeus Mozart (1756 - 1791)

▶ Draw in the missing notes for "Twinkle, Twinkle, Little Star" before you play.

61 GO FOR EXCELLENCE!

KEY SIGNATURE

This key signature means play all B's as B flats, all E's as E flats, and all A's as A flats.

62 CLIMBING STAIRS

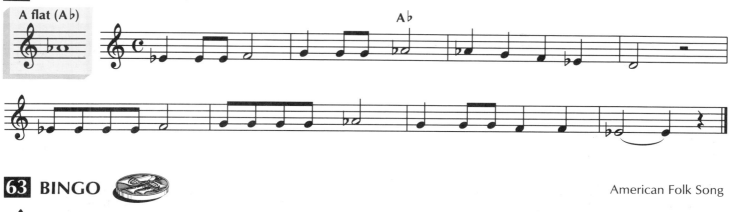

A flat (A♭)

A♭

63 BINGO

American Folk Song

64 THERE'S MUSIC IN THE AIR

George F. Root (1820 - 1895)

65 THERE'S THE SAME MUSIC IN THE AIR

George F. Root (1820 - 1895)

▶ Circle the notes changed by the key signature.

66 SCALE SKILL   Page 40 ▶

▶ How is your hand position?

67 FOR MALLETS ONLY

DOTTED HALF NOTE

A dot after a note adds half the value of the note.

$\frac{1}{2}$ + • = $\frac{1}{2}$ + $\frac{1}{4}$ = $\frac{1}{2}.$
2 + 1 = 2 + 1 = 3 counts

TIME SIGNATURE $\frac{3}{4}$

$\frac{3}{4}$ = 3 counts in each measure
$\frac{3}{4}$ = quarter note gets 1 count

DYNAMICS

forte (f) - loud
piano (p) - soft

68 WARM-UP

69 CHANNEL THREE

▶ Write in the counting before you play.

70 DOWN IN THE VALLEY   American Mountain Song

71 BROTHER MARTIN - Round   Latin American Folk Song

72 THE LITTLE FISH   Australian Folk Song

▶ Draw in a breath mark at the end of each phrase.

73 GO FOR EXCELLENCE!   Czech Folk Song
"When Love Is Kind"

 **DOTTED HALF NOTE**

A dot after a note adds half the value of the note.

$$\text{half} + \cdot = \text{half} + \text{quarter} = \text{dotted half}$$
$$2 + 1 = 2 + 1 = 3 \text{ counts}$$

TIME SIGNATURE

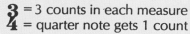 = 3 counts in each measure
= quarter note gets 1 count

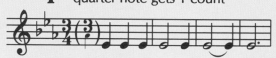

DYNAMICS

forte (*f*) - loud
piano (*p*) - soft

68 WARM-UP

69 CHANNEL THREE

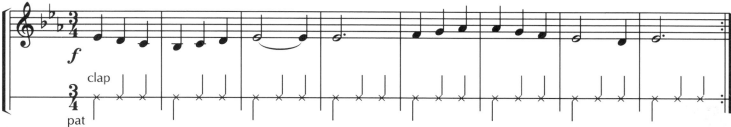

► Write in the counting for the top line before you play.

70 DOWN IN THE VALLEY

American Mountain Song

71 BROTHER MARTIN - Round

Latin American Folk Song

72 THE LITTLE FISH   Page 40 ▌▌▌▶

Australian Folk Song

► Draw in a breath mark at the end of each phrase.

73 GO FOR EXCELLENCE!

Czech Folk Song

"When Love Is Kind"

▶ When the sticking is in parentheses, move the stick but do not strike the drum head.

NATURAL

A natural sign cancels a flat or a sharp.
It remains in effect for the entire measure.

74 **WARM-UP**

75 **OLD BLUE**

Traditional

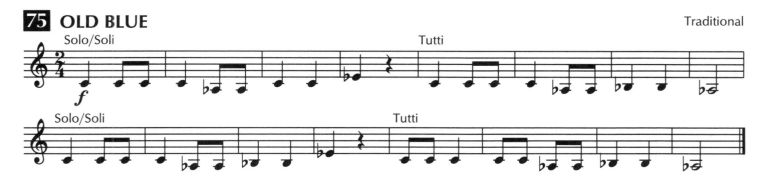

76 **THIRD TIME AROUND**

▶ Circle the notes changed by the key signature.

77 **LULLABY - Duet**

Traditional

78 **MINUTEMAN MARCH**

Robert Frost (b. 1942)

also played A♮

79 **FOR MALLETS ONLY**

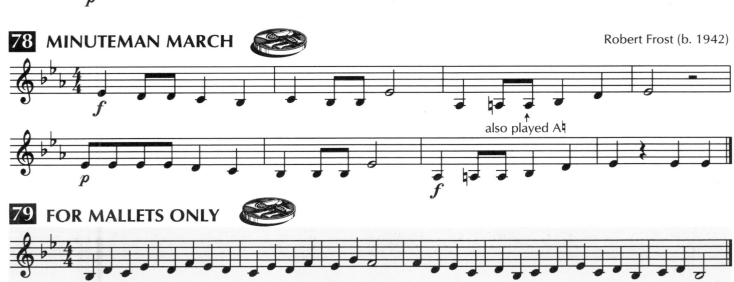

1st and 2nd ENDINGS

Play the first ending the first time through. Then, repeat the music, skip the first ending, and play the second ending.

80 MEXICAN HAT DANCE

Mexican Folk Song

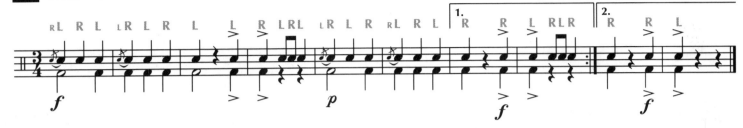

81 FRÈRE JACQUES - Round

Page 40

French Folk Song

82 MORNING MOOD

Edvard Grieg (1843 - 1907)

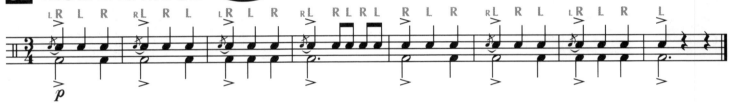

83 MING COURT

Chinese Folk Song

84 GO FOR EXCELLENCE!

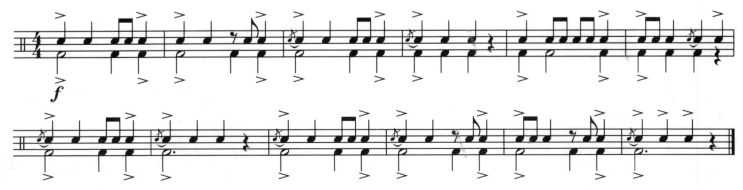

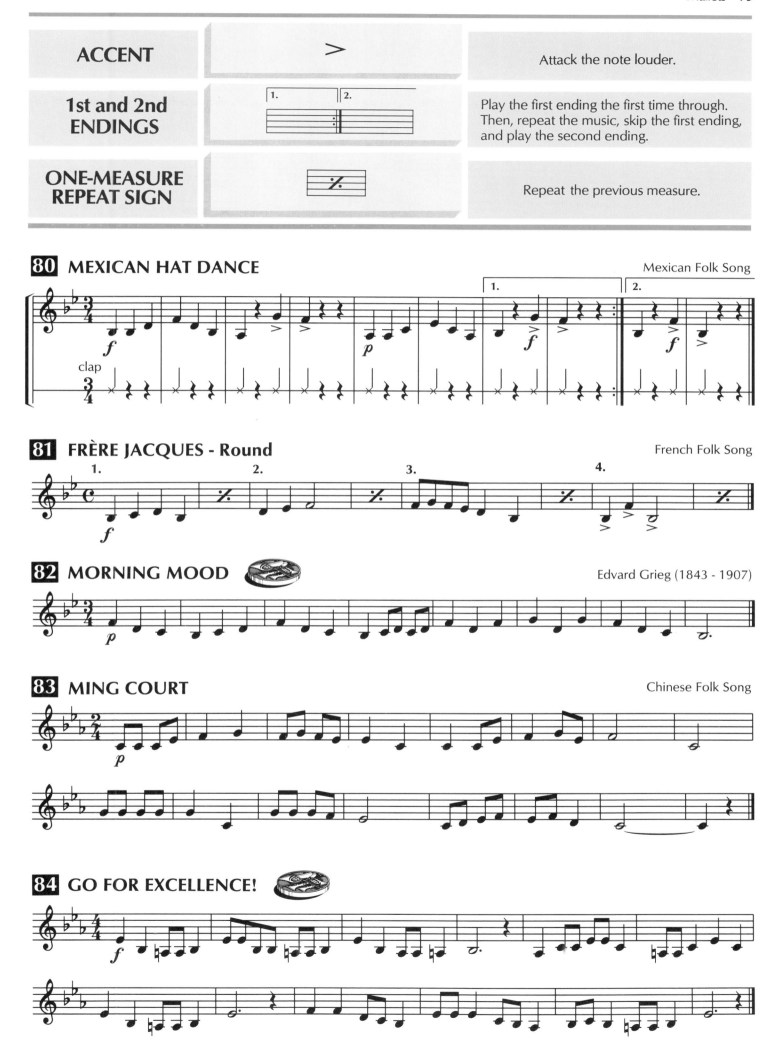

SAWMILL CREEK

Percussion Solo or Ensemble

Bruce Pearson (b. 1942)

▶ Go back to the first repeat sign.

SAWMILL CREEK

Percussion Solo or Ensemble

Bruce Pearson (b. 1942)

▶ Go back to the first repeat sign.

MONTEGO BAY
Band Arrangement

Calypso Song
arr. Chuck Elledge (b. 1961)

REGAL MARCH
Band Arrangement

Bruce Pearson (b. 1942)
arr. Chuck Elledge (b. 1961)

LONG REST

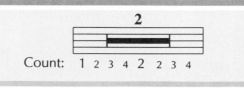

Rest the number of measures indicated.

MONTEGO BAY
Band Arrangement

Calypso Song
arr. Chuck Elledge (b. 1961)

REGAL MARCH
Band Arrangement

Bruce Pearson (b. 1942)
arr. Chuck Elledge (b. 1961)

SIXTEENTH NOTES

Each sixteenth note gets ¼ count in $\frac{2}{4}$, $\frac{3}{4}$, and $\frac{4}{4}$ time.

Two sixteenth notes are as long as one eighth note.
Four sixteenth notes are as long as one quarter note.

$\frac{1}{4} + \frac{1}{4} + \frac{1}{4} + \frac{1}{4} = \frac{1}{2} + \frac{1}{2} = 1$ count

FLAM PARADIDDLE

The flam paradiddle is a Rudiment.

85 WARM-UP

86 FULL OF HOT AIR

87 DANZA GIOVANNI

Italian Folk Song

▶ Write in the counting before you play.

88 B♭ MAJOR SCALE SKILL   Page 40 ▸

Arpeggio

Chords

89 THE MAN ON THE FLYING TRAPEZE

George Leybourne (1842 - 1884)

▶ Go back to the first repeat sign.

90   ▶ See "Mallets" page 22.

91 FOR SNARE DRUMS ONLY

Flam Paradiddle

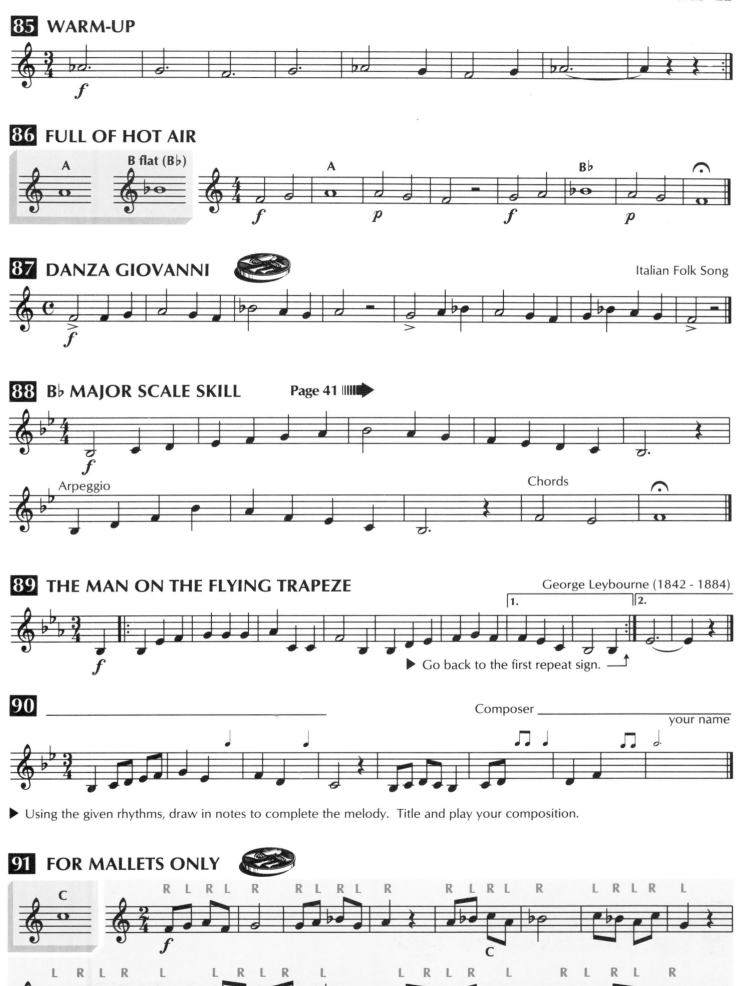

▶ Using the given rhythms, draw in notes to complete the melody. Title and play your composition.

KEY SIGNATURE

This key signature means play all B's as B flats.

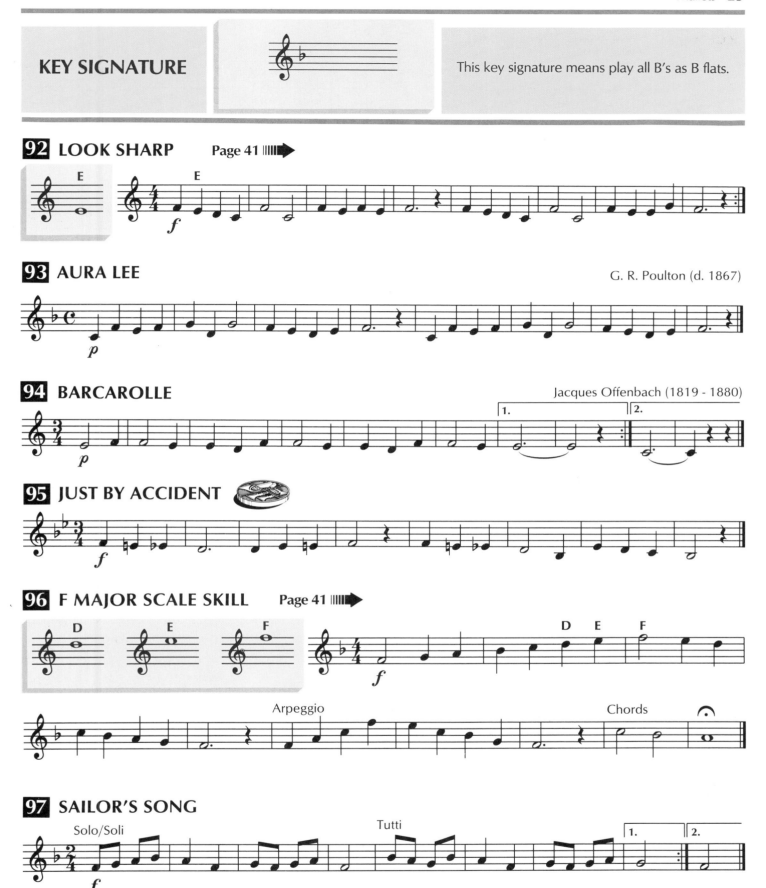

92 LOOK SHARP Page 41

93 AURA LEE G. R. Poulton (d. 1867)

94 BARCAROLLE Jacques Offenbach (1819 - 1880)

95 JUST BY ACCIDENT

96 F MAJOR SCALE SKILL Page 41

Arpeggio · Chords

97 SAILOR'S SONG

Solo/Soli · Tutti

98 GO FOR EXCELLENCE! American Folk Song

"This Old Man"

EIGHTH/SIXTEENTH NOTE COMBINATIONS

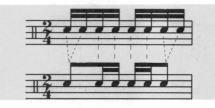

TWO-MEASURE REPEAT SIGN

Repeat the two previous measures.

DA CAPO AL FINE (D. C. AL FINE)

Go back to the beginning and play until the *Fine*.

99 WARM-UP

100 IN THE POCKET/ 101 POCKET CHANGE

102 STRICTLY BUSINESS

103 SMOOTH SAILING

104 ROSES FROM THE SOUTH — Johann Strauss, Jr. (1825 - 1899)

105 THEME FROM "HANSEL AND GRETEL" — Engelbert Humperdinck (1854 - 1921)

106 FOR SNARE DRUMS ONLY

DA CAPO AL FINE (D. C. AL FINE)

Go back to the beginning and play until the *Fine*.

SHARP

A sharp (♯) raises the pitch of a note one half step. It remains in effect for the entire measure.

99 WARM-UP

100 IN THE POCKET

101 POCKET CHANGE

102 STRICTLY BUSINESS

103 SMOOTH SAILING

104 ROSES FROM THE SOUTH

Johann Strauss, Jr. (1825 - 1899)

105 THEME FROM "HANSEL AND GRETEL"

Engelbert Humperdinck (1854 - 1921)

Fine

D.C. al Fine

106 FOR MALLETS ONLY

Page 41

F sharp (F♯)

F♯

also played F♯

107 **THAT'S A WRAP**

108 **POLLY WOLLY DOODLE**

American Folk Song

109 **VOLGA BOAT SONG**

Russian Folk Song

110 **KOOKABURRA - Round**

Marion Sinclair

© 1934 (Renewed) Larrikin Music Pub. Ptg. Ltd.
Administered by Music Sales Corporation, Used by Permission.

111 **GO FOR EXCELLENCE!**

Tielman Susato (1500? - 1561?)

107 THAT'S A WRAP

108 POLLY WOLLY DOODLE

American Folk Song

clap

foot stomp

109 VOLGA BOAT SONG

Russian Folk Song

110 KOOKABURRA - Round

Australian Folk Song

111 GO FOR EXCELLENCE!

Tielman Susato (1500? - 1561?)

"Ronde"

DOTTED QUARTER NOTE

A dot after a note adds half the value of the note.

112 WARM-UP - Band Arrangement

113 SHORT CUT

▶ Write in the counting before you play.

114 SPOT THE DOTS

▶ Feel the pulse of three eighth notes during each dotted quarter note.

115 ALL THROUGH THE NIGHT

Welsh Folk Song

116 ALOUETTE

French–Canadian Folk Song

117 FOR SNARE DRUMS ONLY

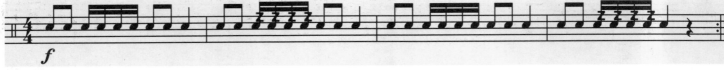

SINGLE EIGHTH NOTE		A single eighth note is half as long as a quarter note. ♪ = ½ count
DOTTED QUARTER NOTE		A dot after a note adds half the value of the note. ♩ + • = ♩ + ♪ = ♩. 1 + ½ = 1 + ½ = 1 ½ counts
ROLL	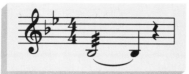	A roll may be used to sustain the sound on a percussion instrument. Use rapid, relaxed <u>single</u> strokes when playing mallet percussion rolls.

112 WARM-UP - Band Arrangement

113 SHORT CUT

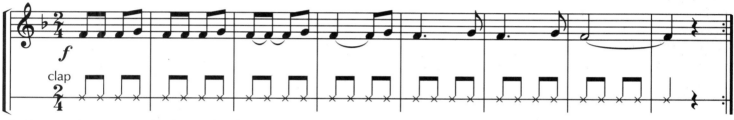

▶ Write in the counting for the top line before you play.

114 SPOT THE DOTS

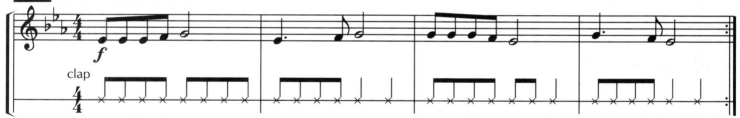

▶ Feel the pulse of three eighth notes during each dotted quarter note.

115 ALL THROUGH THE NIGHT

Welsh Folk Song

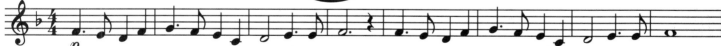

116 ALOUETTE

French-Canadian Folk Song

117 FOR MALLETS ONLY

NINE STROKE ROLL (QUARTER NOTE ROLL)

written: primary strokes: played:

The nine stroke roll is a Rudiment. A roll may be used to sustain the sound on a percussion instrument.

118 JUST A LITTLE OFF THE TOP

119 TOP DRAWER - Duet Page 41 ▶

120 HOME ON THE RANGE

Daniel E. Kelley (1843 - 1905)

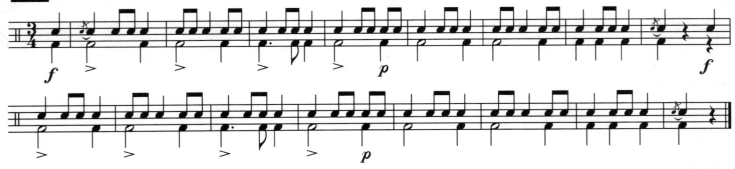

121 THE CONQUERING HERO - Duet

George Frideric Handel (1685 - 1759)

122 GO FOR EXCELLENCE!

118 JUST A LITTLE OFF THE TOP

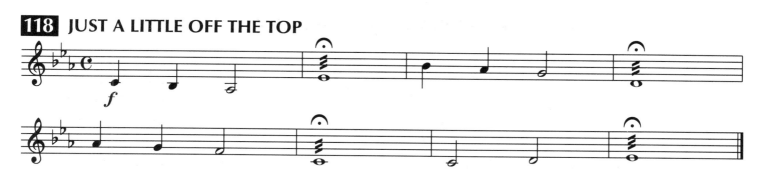

119 TOP DRAWER - Duet   Page 41 ▶

120 HOME ON THE RANGE

Daniel E. Kelley (1843 - 1905)

▶ Circle the notes changed by the key signature.

121 THE CONQUERING HERO - Duet

George Frideric Handel (1685 - 1759)

122 GO FOR EXCELLENCE!

| TEMPOS | **Andante** - moderately slow
Moderato - moderate speed
Allegro - quick and lively | DYNAMICS | *mezzo forte* (*mf*) - medium loud |

FIVE STROKE ROLL (EIGHTH NOTE ROLL)

The five stroke roll is a Rudiment.

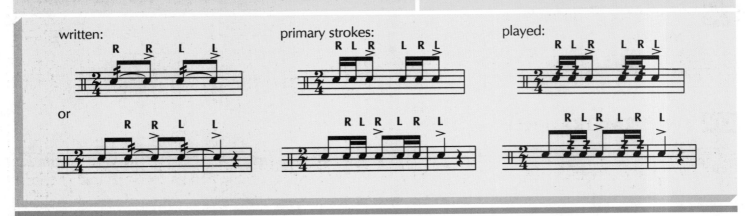

123 WARM-UP - Band Arrangement

Andante

124 HIGH WINDS AHEAD

Andante

125 LOOK BEFORE YOU LEAP

Moderato

126 E♭ MAJOR SCALE SKILL

Allegro

Arpeggio

127 VARIATIONS ON A THEME BY MOZART   ▶ See "Mallets" page 28.

128 FOR SNARE DRUMS ONLY

Andante

TEMPOS
Andante - moderately slow
Moderato - moderate speed
Allegro - quick and lively

DYNAMICS
mezzo forte (***mf***) - medium loud
mezzo piano (***mp***) - medium soft

123 WARM-UP - Band Arrangement
Andante

124 HIGH WINDS AHEAD
Andante

125 LOOK BEFORE YOU LEAP Page 41
Moderato

126 E♭ MAJOR SCALE SKILL
E flat (E♭)
Allegro
E♭
Arpeggio
Chords

127 VARIATIONS ON A THEME BY MOZART
Wolfgang Amadeus Mozart (1756 – 1791)
Moderato
Theme (main melody)
Variation 1 (time signature changes)
Variation 2 (rhythm changes)
Variation 3 (melody changes)

128 FOR MALLETS ONLY
Andante
R R R R R R R R R L L L L L L L L L

W21PR

BALANCE BUILDER

TRUMPET VOLUNTARY
Band Arrangement

Jeremiah Clarke (1674? - 1707)
arr. Bruce Pearson (b. 1942)

Moderato

BALANCE BUILDER

TRUMPET VOLUNTARY
Band Arrangement

Jeremiah Clarke (1674? - 1707)
arr. Bruce Pearson (b. 1942)

TEMPO	*Ritardando (**ritard.** or **rit.**)* - Gradually slow the tempo.

135 **SAKURA - Duet**

Japanese Folk Song

▶ Draw in a breath mark at the end of each phrase.

136 **GRANDFATHER'S WHISKERS**

American Folk Song

137 **TWINKLE VARIATION** ▶ See "Mallets" page 31.

TEMPO	*Ritardando (ritard.* or *rit.)* - Gradually slow the tempo.

135 **SAKURA - Duet**   Japanese Folk Song
Andante

▶ Draw in a breath mark at the end of each phrase.

136 **GRANDFATHER'S WHISKERS**   American Folk Song
Moderato

137 **TWINKLE VARIATION**   Wolfgang Amadeus Mozart (1756 – 1791)
Theme

Composer Viviane Ly
                                                          your name

Variation

▶ Compose a variation on "Twinkle, Twinkle, Little Star."

b♭c b♭c   FF   G♭ F   E E D D   C D C   B♭   W21PR

SEVENTEEN STROKE ROLL (HALF NOTE ROLL)

The seventeen stroke roll is a Rudiment.

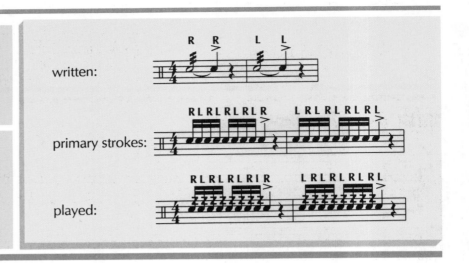

written:

primary strokes:

played:

138 PARTNER SONGS - Duet

American Spirituals

Andante

"Swing Low, Sweet Chariot"/ "All Night, All Day"

139 MANHATTAN BEACH MARCH

John Philip Sousa (1854 - 1932)

Allegro

Introduction

Theme

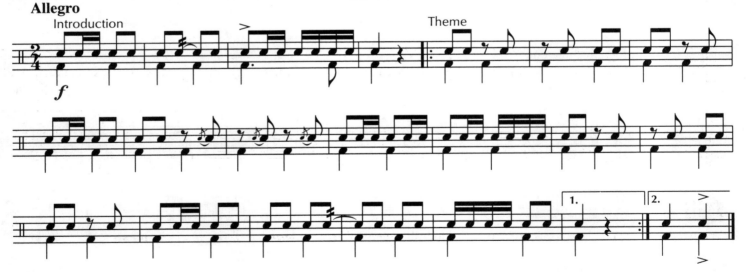

140 DYNAMIC DECISION ▶ See "Mallets" page 32.

141 FOR SNARE DRUMS ONLY

Moderato

DOUBLE STOP

Two notes played at the same time by one player.

138 PARTNER SONGS - Duet

American Spirituals

Andante

"Swing Low, Sweet Chariot"

"All Night, All Day"

139 MANHATTAN BEACH MARCH

John Philip Sousa (1854 - 1932)

Allegro

Introduction

Theme

140 DYNAMIC DECISION

Write in the following dynamics from softest to loudest: *mezzo forte*   *piano*   *forte*   *mezzo piano*

_____   _____   _____   _____

softest ⟵   ⟶ loudest

141 FOR MALLETS ONLY

Moderato

▶ Play this exercise using double stops.

TEMPO	Largo - slow

142 "LARGO" FROM THE NEW WORLD SYMPHONY Antonin Dvořák (1841 - 1904)

143 JUST FINE Page 41

144 CHORALE - Duet Lowell Mason (1792 - 1872)

145 TEMPO TIME ▶ See "Mallets" page 33.

146 GO FOR EXCELLENCE!

TEMPO	Largo - slow

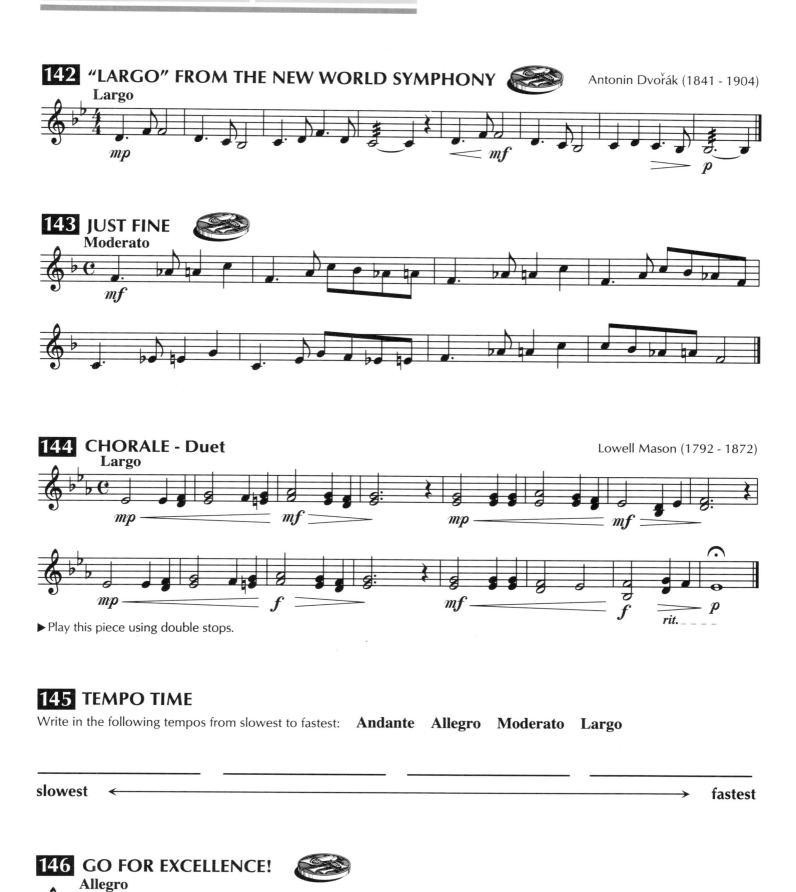

142 **"LARGO" FROM THE NEW WORLD SYMPHONY**   Antonin Dvořák (1841 - 1904)

Largo

mp   *mf*   *p*

143 **JUST FINE**

Moderato

mf

144 **CHORALE - Duet**   Lowell Mason (1792 - 1872)

Largo

mp   mf   mp   mf

mp   f   mf   f   p

rit.

▶ Play this piece using double stops.

145 **TEMPO TIME**

Write in the following tempos from slowest to fastest: **Andante   Allegro   Moderato   Largo**

_____   _____   _____   _____

slowest ←   → fastest

146 **GO FOR EXCELLENCE!**

Allegro

mf

147 **RICOCHET ROCK**

Chuck Elledge (b. 1961)

148 **LOCH LOMOND** Page 41

Scottish Folk Song

149 **SHALOM, CHAVERIM**

Hebrew Folk Song

▶ Draw in a breath mark at the end of each phrase.

150 _____ Composer _____
your name

▶ Compose an ending for this song. Title and play your composition.

151 **FOR SNARE DRUMS ONLY**

147 RICOCHET ROCK

Chuck Elledge (b. 1961)

Allegro

148 LOCH LOMOND

Scottish Folk Song

Moderato

149 SHALOM, CHAVERIM

Hebrew Folk Song

Andante

▶ Draw in a breath mark at the end of each phrase.

150 _____ Composer _____

your name

▶ Compose an ending for this melody. Title and play your composition.

151 FOR MALLETS ONLY

Moderato

152 GRANDFATHER'S CLOCK

Henry C. Work (1832 - 1884)

153 KUM BA YAH

African Folk Song

154 GRANT US PEACE - Round

German Canon

155 GO FOR EXCELLENCE!

152 GRANDFATHER'S CLOCK Page 41 ⏩

Henry C. Work (1832 - 1884)

▶ Circle the note changed by the key signature.

153 KUM BA YAH

African Folk Song

154 GRANT US PEACE - Round

German Canon

155 GO FOR EXCELLENCE!

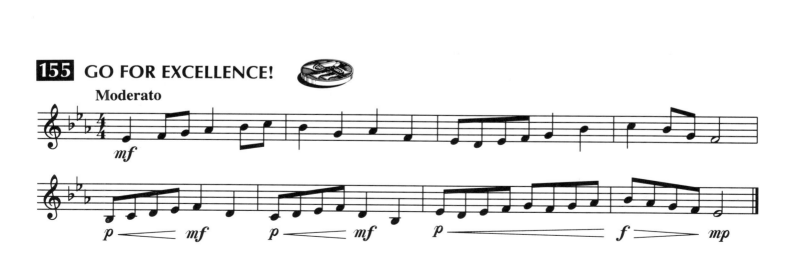

THE ROYAL DRUMMER

Snare Drum / Bass Drum Duet

Bruce Pearson (b. 1942)

RIM SHOT (R.S.)

Place tip of one stick on the head of the drum. Strike the shaft of that stick with the shaft of the other stick.

STICKING WITH IT
Multiple Percussion Solo

Bruce Pearson (b. 1942)

W21PR

MINUET
Solo with Piano Accompaniment

Johann Sebastian Bach
(1685 - 1750)

LONG REST

Count: 1 2 3 4 2 2 3 4

Rest the number of measures indicated.

ROCKIN' RONDEAU
Band Arrangement

Based on a theme by
Jean-Joseph Mouret (1682 – 1738)
arr. Chuck Elledge (b. 1961)

▶ The snare drum and suspended cymbal may be played by one percussionist. See page 2 of the *Standard of Excellence* Timpani & Auxiliary Percussion book for information on playing suspended cymbal.

ROCKIN' RONDEAU
Band Arrangement

Based on a theme by
Jean-Joseph Mouret (1682 – 1738)
arr. Chuck Elledge (b. 1961)

⏩ EXCELLERATORS - FOR SNARE DRUMS ONLY

EXCELLERATORS-FOR SNARE DRUMS ONLY

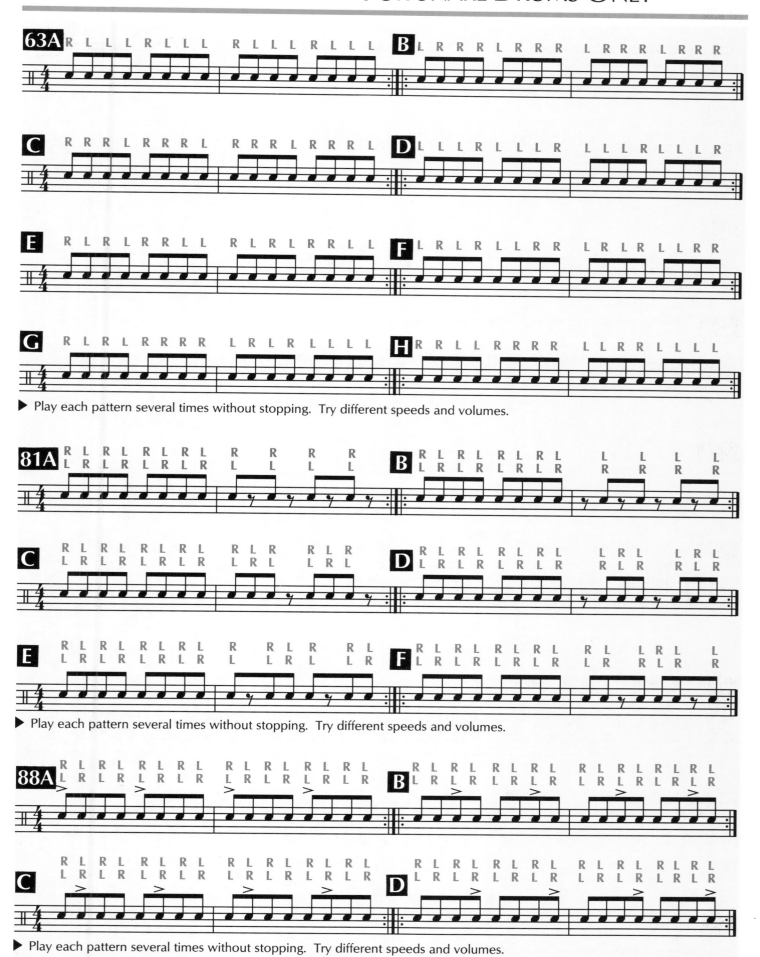

▶ Play each pattern several times without stopping. Try different speeds and volumes.

▶ Play each pattern several times without stopping. Try different speeds and volumes.

▶ Play each pattern several times without stopping. Try different speeds and volumes.

EXCELLERATORS- FOR SNARE DRUMS ONLY

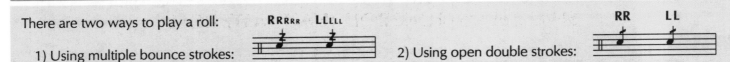

There are two ways to play a roll:

1) Using multiple bounce strokes:

2) Using open double strokes:

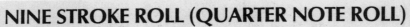

The multiple bounce stroke roll is used for most concert band, orchestra, and ensemble playing. The double stroke open roll is used primarily in marches and in marching band. In this book, rolls may be played either way.

NINE STROKE ROLL (QUARTER NOTE ROLL)

FIVE STROKE ROLL (EIGHTH NOTE ROLL)

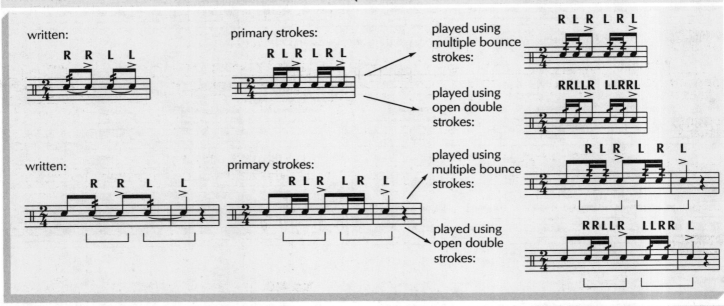

EXCELLERATORS- FOR SNARE DRUMS ONLY

SEVENTEEN STROKE ROLL (HALF NOTE ROLL)

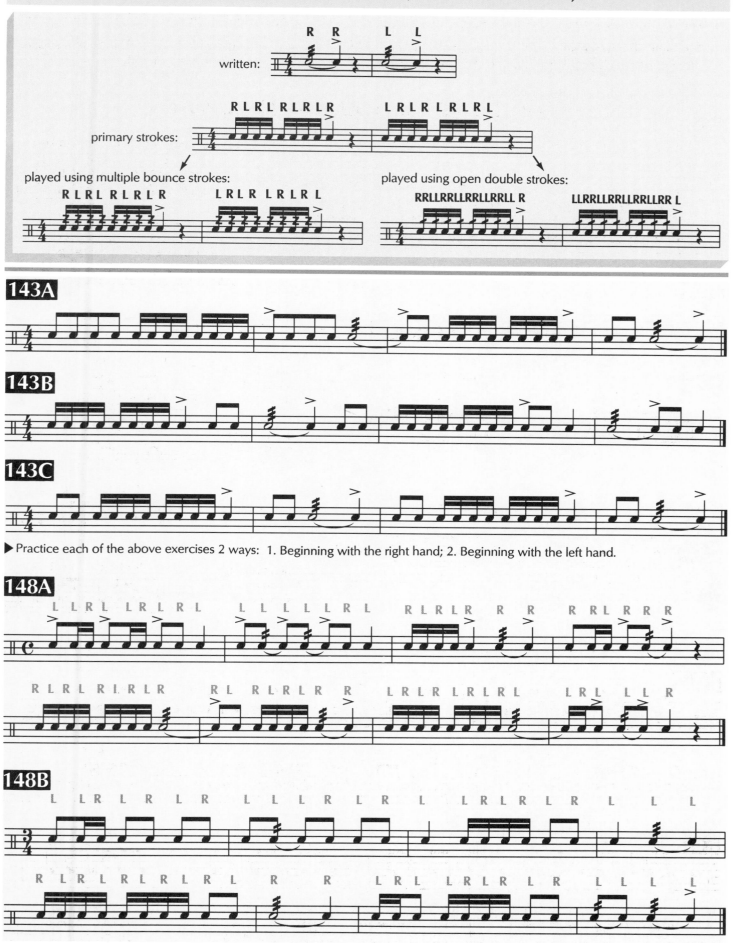

▶ Practice each of the above exercises 2 ways: 1. Beginning with the right hand; 2. Beginning with the left hand.

⮕ EXCELLERATORS - FOR MALLETS ONLY

4A

▶ Use alternate sticking (**R-L-R-L** or **L-R-L-R**).

4B

12A

12B

23A

23B

▶ Try different stickings.

EXCELLERATORS- FOR MALLETS ONLY

▶ Double stickings may be used for consecutive notes.

▶ Keep your left hand on B♭.

EXCELLERATORS - FOR MALLETS ONLY

88A

▶ Try different stickings.

88B

92

96A

▶ Keep your left hand on F. Also try playing this exercise with your right hand or left hand only.

96B

106

▶ Try using double stickings.

EXCELLERATORS - FOR MALLETS ONLY

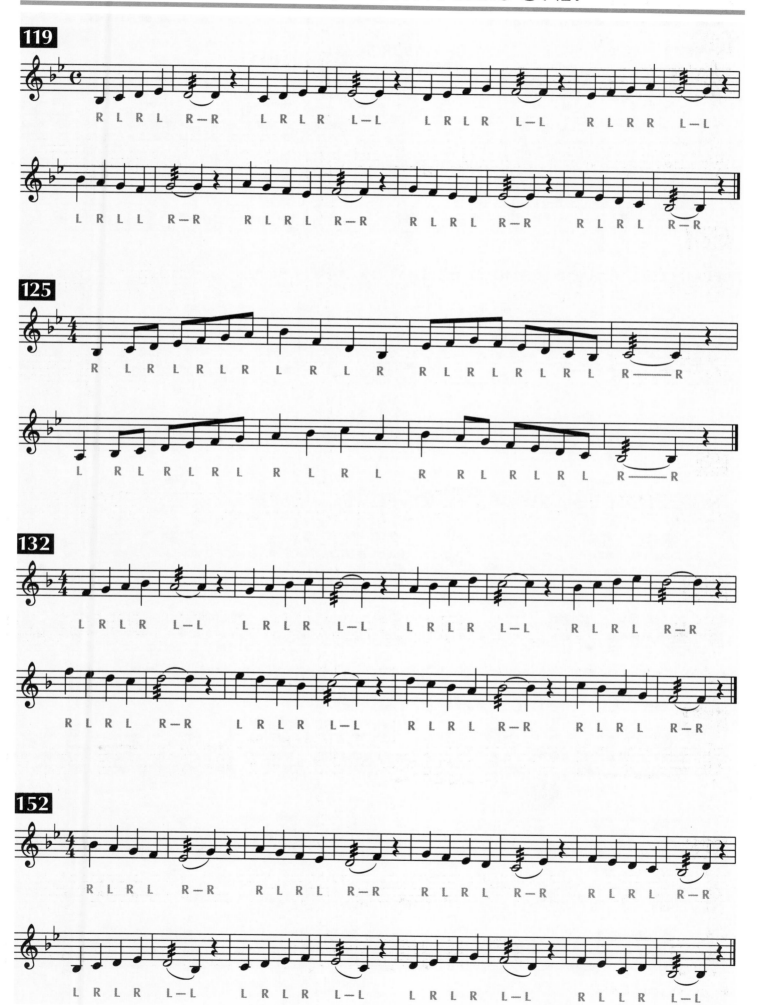

RUDIMENT STUDIES (SCALE STUDIES)

SINGLE PARADIDDLE STUDY (B♭ MAJOR SCALE)

FLAM TAP / FLAM PARADIDDLE STUDY (E♭ MAJOR SCALE)

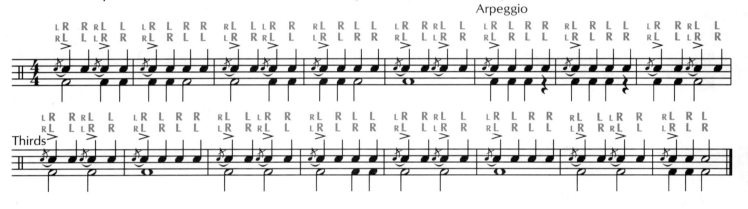

NINE STROKE ROLL STUDY (F MAJOR SCALE)

FIVE STROKE ROLL STUDY (A♭ MAJOR SCALE)

SEVENTEEN STROKE ROLL STUDY (CHROMATIC SCALE)

SCALE STUDIES

Bb MAJOR SCALE

Eb MAJOR SCALE

F MAJOR SCALE

Ab MAJOR SCALE

CHROMATIC SCALE

RHYTHM STUDIES

RHYTHM STUDIES

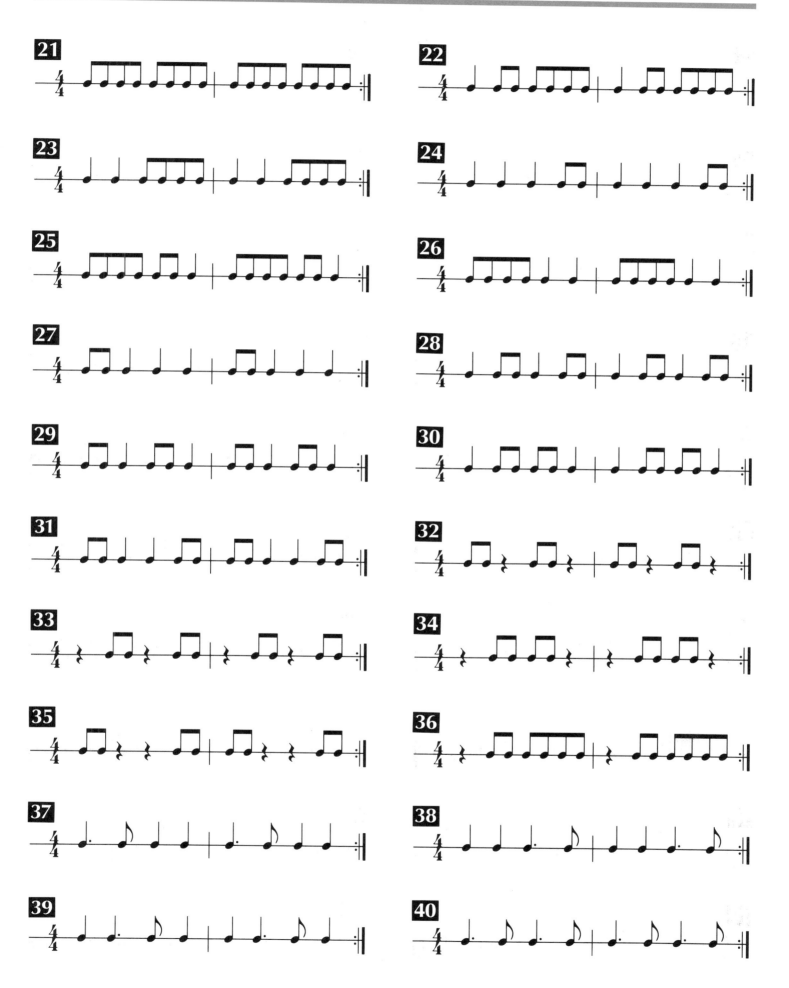

RHYTHM STUDIES

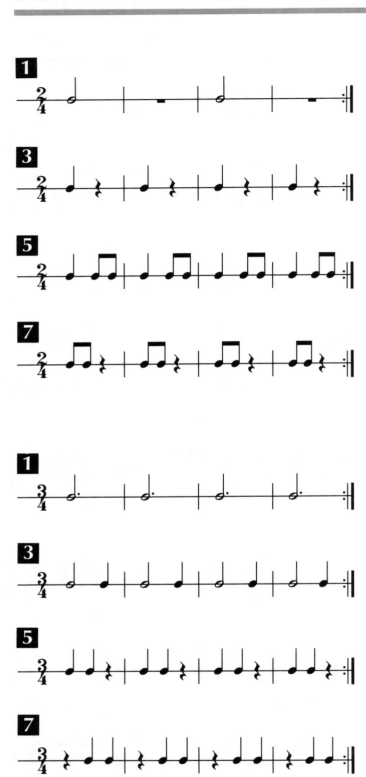
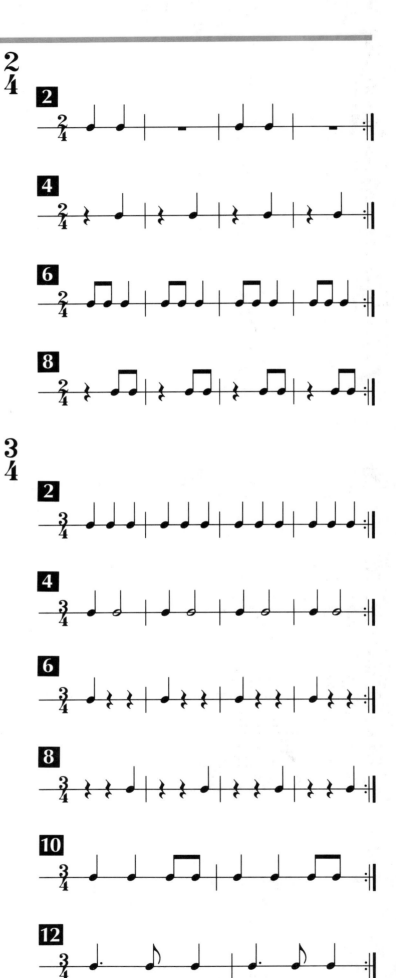

ADVANCED RHYTHM STUDIES

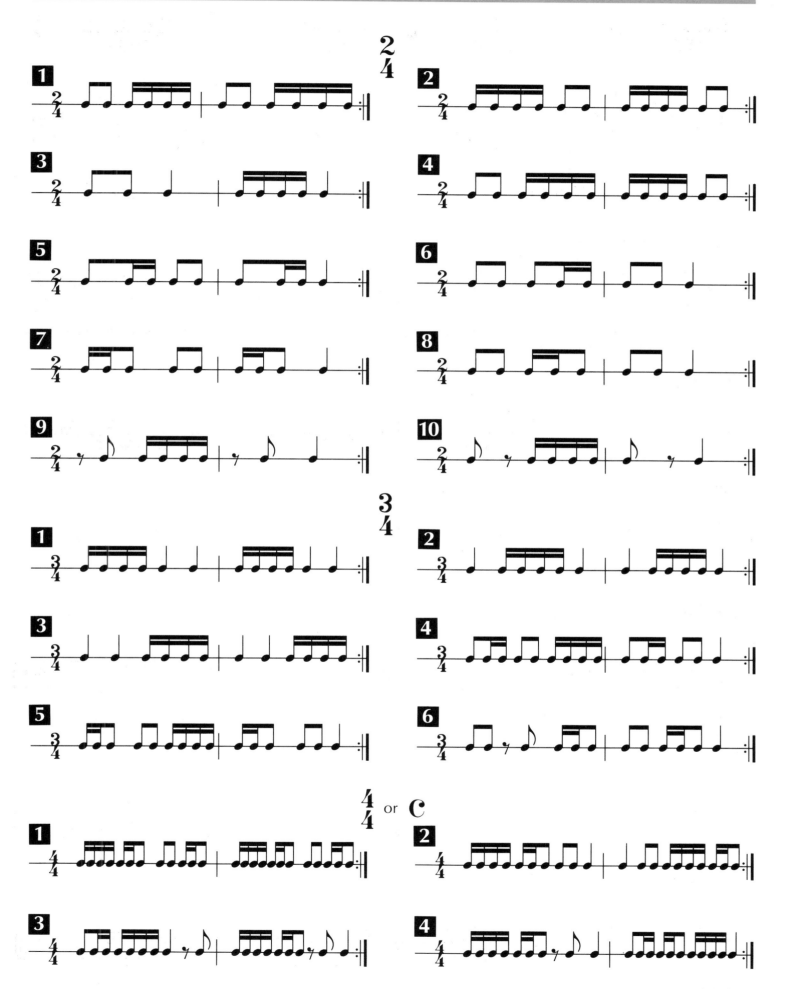

GLOSSARY/INDEX

▶ D = Drum page, M = Mallet page

Multiple Bounce Stroke (pp.9D,41D) . . type of stroke that produces three or more sounds (hits) with a single wrist movement; the first hit is the strongest, with the others gradually decreasing in intensity

Multiple Bounce Stroke Roll (pp.41D, 48D) . . . . roll played using multiple bounce strokes; used for most concert band, orchestra, and ensemble playing; also called buzz roll, press roll, closed roll, concert roll, and orchestral roll

Natural (p.18M) ♮ . . . . cancels a flat or sharp

Nine Stroke Roll (Quarter Note Roll) (pp.27D, 41D, 48D) . . . . a rudiment; when played using open double strokes, a total of 9 strokes are produced

Offenbach, Jacques (p.23) . . . . French composer (1819-1880)

One-Measure Repeat Sign (pp.12D, 19M) . . . . repeat the previous measure

Open Double Stroke (p.41D) . . . . type of stroke that produces two sounds (hits) with a single wrist movement; both hits should sound the same

Orchestra Bells (see **Bells**)

Orchestral Roll (see **Multiple Bounce Stroke Roll**)

Paradiddle, Single (see **Single Paradiddle**)

Pearson, Bruce . . . . American composer/author (b. 1942)

Percussion Clef (pp.4D, 6D) . . . . . . indicates that the lines and spaces on the staff do not designate specific pitches; also called neutral clef or no-pitch clef; read by snare drum, bass drum, cymbals, and most other auxiliary percussion instruments

Phrase (p.8) . . . . musical thought or sentence

Piano (p.17) *p* . . . . soft

Pick-Up Note(s) (p.15) . . . . . note or notes that come before first full measure

Pierpont, J. S. (p.12) . . . . . American composer (1822-1893)

Poulton, G.R. (p.23) . . . . . . American composer (d.1867)

Press Roll (see **Multiple Bounce Stroke Roll**)

Quarter Note Roll (see **Nine Stroke Roll**)

Repeat Sign (pp.9, 20) . . . . repeat from beginning or repeat section of music between repeat signs

Resonator (Resonating Tube) (p.48M) . . . . on a mallet instrument, a tube which naturally amplifies the volume and enriches the sound of a vibrating bar after the bar is struck

Rim Shot (R.S.) (p.37D) . . . . special effect played on a drum; to create, place the tip of one stick on the drum head; strike the shaft of that stick with the shaft of the other stick

Ritardando (ritard. or rit.) (p.31) . . . gradually slow the tempo

Roll (pp.26M, 27-28D, 32D, 41D, 48D) technique that may be used to sustain the sound on a percussion instrument

Root, George F. (p.16) . . . . American composer/publisher (1820-1895)

Rossini, Gioacchino (p.13) . . . . . . Italian composer (1792-1868)

Rudiment (pp.8D, 11-12D, 18D, 22D, 27-28D, 32D, 41-42D, 48D) . . 40 basic techniques and sticking patterns used in snare drum playing

Scale (pp.22-23, 28, 42) . . . . collection of pitches arranged from lowest to highest or highest to lowest

Seventeen Stroke Roll (Half Note Roll) (pp.32D, 41D, 48D) . . . . . a rudiment; when played using open double strokes, a total of 17 strokes are produced

Sharp (p.24M) ♯ . . . . raises the pitch of a note ½ step

Single Paradiddle (pp.8D, 48D) . . . . a rudiment; consists of two alternating strokes followed by two strokes played by the same hand

Snares Off (pp.10-11D, 16D, 19-20D, 25D, 31D, 34-35D, 37D) . . . . an instruction to move the snare release lever (p.2D) so snares are not touching the snare head

Soli (p.9) . . . . whole section plays

Solo (p.9) . . . . one person plays

Sousa, John Philip (p.32) . . . . American composer (1854-1932)

Staff (pp.4, 6) . . . . lines and spaces on which music is written

Sticking (pp.4, 6) . . . . pattern of right (**R**) and left (**L**) hand strokes used to play a piece of percussion music

Strauss, Johann Jr. (p.24) . . . . Austrian composer (1825-1899)

Subdominant (pp.12, 30) . . . . fourth note of a scale; chord built on fourth note of a scale

Susato, Tielman (p.25) . . . . Belgian composer (1500?-1561?)

Tempo (pp.28, 31, 33) . . . . speed of music

Theme (pp.28, 31M, 32) . . . . main musical idea in a piece of music

Tie (p.10) . . . . curved line that connects two notes of the same pitch; tied notes are played as one unbroken note

Time Signature (pp.4, 6, 9-10, 17) . . . top number tells you number of counts in each measure; bottom number tells you the type of note that receives one count

Tonic (pp.12, 30) . . . . first note of a scale; chord built on first note of a scale

Treble Clef (pp.4M, 6M) . . . . G Clef; read by flute, oboe, clarinets, saxophones, trumpet, french horn & mallet percussion

Tubular Bells (see **Chimes**)

Tutti (p.9) . . . . everyone plays

Two-Measure Repeat Sign (p.24D) . . . repeat the two previous measures

Variation (pp.28, 31M) . . . . repeated musical idea which has been slightly changed in some way from the original

Vibraphone (p.48M) . . . . mallet percussion instrument with metal bars, a resonating tube under each bar, a damper pedal, and a motor- rotated disk in each resonator which creates a vibrato effect; also called vibes or vibraharp

Vibraharp (see **Vibraphone**)

Vibes (see **Vibraphone**)

Work, Henry C. (p.35) . . . . American composer (1832-1884)

Xylophone (p.48M) . . . . mallet percussion instrument with wooden or synthetic bars, and usually a resonating tube under each bar

W21PR

STANDARD OF EXCELLENCE

Use this chart to record your progress on the "Drums" pages.

EXERCISE 7
- [ ] rhythm
- [ ] sticking
- [ ] grip

EXERCISE 12
- [ ] rhythm
- [ ] sticking
- [ ] accents

EXERCISE 14
- [ ] rhythm
- [ ] sticking
- [ ] accents

EXERCISE 17
- [ ] rhythm
- [ ] sticking
- [ ] accents

EXERCISE 22
- [ ] rhythm
- [ ] sticking
- [ ] paradiddles

EXERCISE 23
- [ ] rhythm
- [ ] mult. bounce
- [ ] repeat

EXERCISE 29
- [ ] rhythm
- [ ] B.D. tech.
- [ ] mult. bounce

EXERCISE 31
- [ ] rhythm
- [ ] pulse
- [ ] mult. bounce

EXERCISE 35
- [ ] rhythm
- [ ] pulse
- [ ] mult. bounce

EXERCISE 39
- [ ] rhythm
- [ ] flams
- [ ] mult. bounce

EXERCISE 41
- [ ] rhythm
- [ ] flams
- [ ] paradiddles

EXERCISE 43
- [ ] rhythm
- [ ] mult. bounce
- [ ] flam taps

EXERCISE 46
- [ ] rhythm
- [ ] sticking
- [ ] stroke

EXERCISE 49
- [ ] rhythm
- [ ] pulse
- [ ] mult. bounce

EXERCISE 53
- [ ] rhythm
- [ ] pulse
- [ ] stroke

EXERCISE 55
- [ ] rhythm
- [ ] flams
- [ ] stroke

EXERCISE 57
- [ ] rhythm
- [ ] pulse
- [ ] stroke

EXERCISE 61
- [ ] rhythm
- [ ] flams
- [ ] paradiddles

EXERCISE 63
- [ ] rhythm
- [ ] flams
- [ ] grip

EXERCISE 67
- [ ] rhythm
- [ ] pulse
- [ ] mult. bounce

EXERCISE 70
- [ ] rhythm
- [ ] sticking
- [ ] dynamics

EXERCISE 73
- [ ] rhythm
- [ ] flams
- [ ] dynamics

EXERCISE 78
- [ ] rhythm
- [ ] flams
- [ ] mult. bounce

EXERCISE 79
- [ ] rhythm
- [ ] pulse
- [ ] sticking

EXERCISE 82
- [ ] rhythm
- [ ] accents
- [ ] flam accents

EXERCISE 84
- [ ] rhythm
- [ ] grip
- [ ] flam accents

EXERCISE 87
- [ ] rhythm
- [ ] sticking
- [ ] accents

EXERCISE 91
- [ ] rhythm
- [ ] flam parads.
- [ ] grip

EXERCISE 95
- [ ] rhythm
- [ ] accents
- [ ] flam accents

EXERCISE 98
- [ ] rhythm
- [ ] mult. bounce
- [ ] flam parads.

EXERCISE 104
- [ ] rhythm
- [ ] B. D. tech.
- [ ] dynamics

EXERCISE 106
- [ ] rhythm
- [ ] sticking
- [ ] stroke

EXERCISE 111
- [ ] rhythm
- [ ] flams
- [ ] dynamics

EXERCISE 115
- [ ] rhythm
- [ ] mult. bounce
- [ ] B. D. tech.

EXERCISE 117
- [ ] rhythm
- [ ] pulse
- [ ] mult. bounce

EXERCISE 122
- [ ] rhythm
- [ ] flams
- [ ] B. D. tech.

EXERCISE 126
- [ ] rhythm
- [ ] 9 stroke rolls
- [ ] tempo

EXERCISE 128
- [ ] rhythm
- [ ] 5 stroke rolls
- [ ] tempo

EXERCISE 131
- [ ] rhythm
- [ ] flam parads.
- [ ] dynamics

EXERCISE 134
- [ ] rhythm
- [ ] 5 stroke rolls
- [ ] 9 stroke rolls

EXERCISE 136
- [ ] rhythm
- [ ] 5 stroke rolls
- [ ] 9 stroke rolls

EXERCISE 139
- [ ] rhythm
- [ ] pulse
- [ ] repeat

EXERCISE 141
- [ ] rhythm
- [ ] sticking
- [ ] 17 stroke rolls

EXERCISE 142
- [ ] rhythm
- [ ] dynamics
- [ ] tempo

EXERCISE 143
- [ ] rhythm
- [ ] 17 stroke rolls
- [ ] tempo

EXERCISE 146
- [ ] rhythm
- [ ] 5 stroke rolls
- [ ] 17 stroke roll

EXERCISE 148
- [ ] rhythm
- [ ] 17 stroke roll
- [ ] dynamics

EXERCISE 151
- [ ] rhythm
- [ ] accents
- [ ] grip

EXERCISE 153
- [ ] rhythm
- [ ] stroke
- [ ] B. D. tech.

EXERCISE 155
- [ ] rhythm
- [ ] 5 stroke rolls
- [ ] 9 stroke rolls

STANDARD OF EXCELLENCE

EXERCISE 7 — ☐ notes ☐ rhythm ☐ grip
EXERCISE 12 — ☐ notes ☐ rhythm ☐ sticking
EXERCISE 14 — ☐ notes ☐ rhythm ☐ sticking
EXERCISE 17 — ☐ notes ☐ rhythm ☐ sticking
EXERCISE 22 — ☐ notes ☐ rhythm ☐ sticking

EXERCISE 23 — ☐ notes ☐ rhythm ☐ repeat
EXERCISE 29 — ☐ notes ☐ rhythm ☐ stroke
EXERCISE 31 — ☐ notes ☐ rhythm ☐ stroke
EXERCISE 35 — ☐ notes ☐ rhythm ☐ sticking
EXERCISE 39 — ☐ notes ☐ rhythm ☐ pulse

EXERCISE 41 — ☐ notes ☐ rhythm ☐ repeat
EXERCISE 43 — ☐ notes ☐ rhythm ☐ sticking
EXERCISE 46 — ☐ notes ☐ rhythm ☐ sticking
EXERCISE 49 — ☐ notes ☐ rhythm ☐ pulse
EXERCISE 53 — ☐ notes ☐ rhythm ☐ pulse

EXERCISE 55 — ☐ notes ☐ rhythm ☐ sticking
EXERCISE 57 — ☐ notes ☐ rhythm ☐ pulse
EXERCISE 61 — ☐ notes ☐ rhythm ☐ stroke
EXERCISE 63 — ☐ notes ☐ rhythm ☐ pulse
EXERCISE 67 — ☐ notes ☐ rhythm ☐ sticking

EXERCISE 70 — ☐ notes ☐ rhythm ☐ dynamics
EXERCISE 73 — ☐ notes ☐ rhythm ☐ sticking
EXERCISE 78 — ☐ notes ☐ rhythm ☐ stroke
EXERCISE 79 — ☐ notes ☐ rhythm ☐ sticking
EXERCISE 82 — ☐ notes ☐ rhythm ☐ sticking

EXERCISE 84 — ☐ notes ☐ rhythm ☐ pulse
EXERCISE 87 — ☐ notes ☐ rhythm ☐ accents
EXERCISE 91 — ☐ notes ☐ rhythm ☐ sticking
EXERCISE 95 — ☐ notes ☐ rhythm ☐ sticking
EXERCISE 98 — ☐ notes ☐ rhythm ☐ repeat

EXERCISE 104 — ☐ notes ☐ rhythm ☐ dynamics
EXERCISE 106 — ☐ notes ☐ rhythm ☐ sticking
EXERCISE 111 — ☐ notes ☐ rhythm ☐ sticking
EXERCISE 115 — ☐ notes ☐ rhythm ☐ stroke
EXERCISE 117 — ☐ notes ☐ rhythm ☐ rolls

EXERCISE 122 — ☐ notes ☐ rhythm ☐ sticking
EXERCISE 126 — ☐ notes ☐ rolls ☐ tempo
EXERCISE 128 — ☐ notes ☐ rolls ☐ tempo
EXERCISE 131 — ☐ notes ☐ rhythm ☐ dynamics
EXERCISE 134 — ☐ notes ☐ rhythm ☐ sticking

EXERCISE 136 — ☐ notes ☐ rhythm ☐ sticking
EXERCISE 139 — ☐ notes ☐ rhythm ☐ repeat
EXERCISE 141 — ☐ notes ☐ rhythm ☐ double stops
EXERCISE 142 — ☐ notes ☐ rhythm ☐ tempo
EXERCISE 143 — ☐ notes ☐ rhythm ☐ tempo

EXERCISE 146 — ☐ notes ☐ rhythm ☐ sticking
EXERCISE 148 — ☐ notes ☐ rhythm ☐ dynamics
EXERCISE 151 — ☐ notes ☐ rhythm ☐ double stops
EXERCISE 153 — ☐ notes ☐ rhythm ☐ grip
EXERCISE 155 — ☐ notes ☐ rhythm ☐ sticking

Use this page to record your progress on the "Mallets" pages.

PERCUSSIVE ARTS SOCIETY INTERNATIONAL DRUM RUDIMENTS

▶ All Rudiments should be practiced: *open* (slow) to *close* (fast) to *open* (slow) and/or at an even, moderate march tempo.

I. ROLL RUDIMENTS

A. SINGLE STROKE ROLL RUDIMENTS

1. SINGLE STROKE ROLL*

R L R L R L R L

2. SINGLE STROKE FOUR

R L R L   R L R L
L R L R   L R L R

3. SINGLE STROKE SEVEN

R L R L R L R
L R L R L R L

B. MULTIPLE BOUNCE ROLL RUDIMENTS

4. MULTIPLE BOUNCE ROLL

5. TRIPLE STROKE ROLL

R R R L L L R R R L L L

C. DOUBLE STROKE OPEN ROLL RUDIMENTS

6. DOUBLE STROKE OPEN ROLL*

R R L L R R L L

7. FIVE STROKE ROLL*

R   R L   L

8. SIX STROKE ROLL

R   L R   L
L   R L   R

9. SEVEN STROKE ROLL*

R   L R   L
L   R L   R

10. NINE STROKE ROLL*

R   R   L   L

11. TEN STROKE ROLL*

R   R L   R   R L
L   L R   L   L R

12. ELEVEN STROKE ROLL*

R   R L   R   R L
L   L R   L   L R

13. THIRTEEN STROKE ROLL*

R   R   L   L

14. FIFTEEN STROKE ROLL*

R   L R   L
L   R L   R

15. SEVENTEEN STROKE ROLL
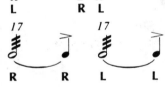
R   R   L   L

II. DIDDLE RUDIMENTS

16. SINGLE PARADIDDLE*

R L R R L R L L

17. DOUBLE PARADIDDLE*

R L R L R R L R L R L L

18. TRIPLE PARADIDDLE

R L R L R L R R L R L R L R L L

19. SINGLE PARADIDDLE-DIDDLE

R L R R L L R L R R L L
L R L L R R L R L L R R

*These Rudiments are also included in the original Standard 26 American Drum Rudiments.

III. FLAM RUDIMENTS

20. FLAM*

L R   r L

21. FLAM ACCENT*

L R L R r L R L

22. FLAM TAP*

L R R r L L L R R r L L

23. FLAMACUE*

L R L R L L R
r L R L R r L

24. FLAM PARADIDDLE*

L R L R R r L R L L

25. SINGLE FLAMMED MILL

L R R L R r L L R L

26. FLAM PARADIDDLE-DIDDLE*

L R L R R L L r L R L L R R

27. PATAFLAFLA

L R L R r L L R L R r L

28. SWISS ARMY TRIPLET

L R R L L r R L
r L L R r L L R

29. INVERTED FLAM TAP

L R L r L R L R L r L R

30. FLAM DRAG

L R L L R r L R R L

IV. DRAG RUDIMENTS

31. DRAG*

LL R   RR L

32. SINGLE DRAG TAP*

LL R L RR L R

33. DOUBLE DRAG TAP*

LL R LL R L RR L RR L R

34. LESSON 25*

LL R L R LL R L R
RR L R L RR L R L

35. SINGLE DRAGADIDDLE

RR L R R LL R L L

36. DRAG PARADIDDLE #1*

R LL R L R R L RR L R L L

37. DRAG PARADIDDLE #2*

R LL R LL R L R R L RR L RR L R L L

38. SINGLE RATAMACUE*

3   3
LL R L R L RR L R L R

39. DOUBLE RATAMACUE*

3   3
LL R LL R L R L RR L RR L R L R

40. TRIPLE RATAMACUE*

3   3
LL R LL R LL R L R L RR L RR L RR L R L R

MALLET PERCUSSION INSTRUMENTS

There are many different types of mallet percussion instruments. The exercises in this book can be played on any of the mallet instruments shown below.

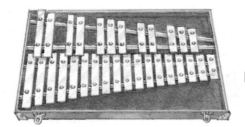

Bells (also called a **glockenspiel** or **orchestra bells**) have metal bars and are played with hard plastic, rubber, or wood mallets.

BELLS

The **marimba** has wooden bars and a resonating tube under each bar. It is played with soft or medium yarn or rubber mallets.

MARIMBA

XYLOPHONE

The **xylophone** has wooden or synthetic bars. It usually also has a resonating tube under each bar. The xylophone is played with rubber, plastic, or wood mallets.

CHIMES

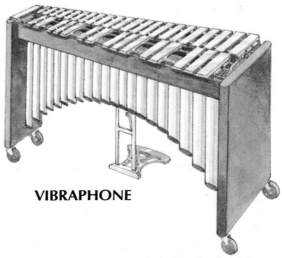

VIBRAPHONE

Chimes (also called **tubular bells**) are long hanging metal tubes, usually supported on a frame. Most sets of chimes also have a damper pedal, used to control ringing. Chimes are played with rawhide, wood, plastic, or hard rubber hammers.

The **vibraphone** (also called **vibes** or **vibraharp**) has metal bars and a resonating tube under each bar. It also has a damper pedal to control the ringing of the bars, and a motor-rotated disk in each resonator which can be used to create a pulsating, vibrato effect. The vibraphone is usually played with rubber or yarn mallets.